The Pleasure Grounds of Suss

Mark Dudeney and Eileen Hallett

With illustrations by Mark Dudeney

Mid-Sussex Books

First published in 2001

Mid-Sussex Books
4 Crescent Road
Burgess Hill
Sussex, RH15 8EG

ISBN 0 9530625 1 1

Printed in Great Britain by
Delta Press, 2 Goldstone Street, Hove, BN3 3RJ

Front cover – Victoria Pleasure Gardens, Burgess Hill
Back cover – Orchard Pleasure Gardens, Hassocks

Acknowledgements

The authors are indebted to the Editor of the Mid Sussex Times and
the Joint Editors and Proprietor of the Hassocks and Keymer Talk
About for permission to quote from their respective publications.

Special thanks are also due to:

QueenSpark Books for allowing us to reproduce a description of the
Orchard Pleasure Gardens that appeared in their publication,
Backyard Brighton.

Mrs Mary Jones, granddaughter of Frederick John Wellman, for
providing us with details of her grandparents' history and photographs
from her family album.

Mr Ray Packham, a good friend whose advice and support has been
greatly appreciated.

Mr Roger Packham, for once again allowing us to use some
photographs from his private collection.

Mr Richard Philcox of the Sussex Archaeological Society.

Mrs Helen Poole, Curator of the Marlipins Museum at Shoreham,
who gave up so much of her time in helping with our researches.

Miss Rose Powell, who was instrumental in providing valuable
information concerning the Orchard Pleasure Gardens and the
Doubleday family.

Other contributors include:

Mr Frederick Avery; the late Cyril Charman; the late George Cragg;
Ms Pat Eatwell; Mrs J. R. Goddard (Secretary of the Sussex Family
History Group); Mr David Grace; Mrs Rhona Green; Mr Dudley
Lipscombe; Mrs Molly Jones; Miss Tina Pierpoint; Mrs Jacqueline
Pollard, Pushkin Books; the late Marjorie Rigold; Mr Charles Smith;
Miss Mary Turton; Mr Alan Upton; Mr Derek Winterburn.

In memory of
Philip Guy Mansfield Dudeney, OBE
and
Boy (Edwin) Upton

Contents

Duck shooting at the Victoria Gardens

Introduction

In our first book, *Edwin Street and the Victoria Pleasure Gardens*, we described the life and times of our grandfather and the pleasure grounds that he opened in Burgess Hill in 1897. Our story ended with his death in 1923, although the Gardens, which were inherited by his daughter, Daisy Upton, continued to function until the outbreak of the Second World War in 1939.

Considerable interest was shown in *Edwin Street and the Victoria Pleasure Gardens*, and it sold out within a year. Since then many people have suggested that we write a sequel covering the final years. It had always been our intention to do so, and the result is here in *The Pleasure Grounds of Sussex*.

In addition to the Burgess Hill Gardens, *The Pleasure Grounds of Sussex* includes the histories of other well known holiday destinations, and in consequence, the reader is provided with a unique viewpoint of bygone days in Sussex.

It should be acknowledged that the establishments included were not the only ones to be found in the county. There were several others, all of which were charming in their different ways. For instance, we have received numerous accounts of the floral delights to be found at Abbotsford, Wannock, and even tiny Litlington (which by some miracle still survives). These, strictly speaking, were Tea Gardens and the extra attractions they boasted – apart from the beauty of their surroundings – were purely incidental, and not the primary reason for paying a visit.

The resorts which we describe were quite different affairs, and catered for the masses. They were the package holidays of their time, and offered a variety of activities for everybody. They also offered subsidised transportation initially, in the form of horse-drawn buses, then later, by the provision of charabancs and special excursion trains.

Throughout the nineteenth as well as part of the twentieth centuries, such Gardens provided virtually the only opportunity that existed for an organised family day out. Little has, up to now, been recorded about them and knowledge of the subject is scarce. We therefore invite the reader to accompany us on a journey back through time, and with the assistance of prints and old photographs to discover how our ancestors whiled away their leisure hours.

Lads boating in the Victoria Pleasure Gardens in the 1930s

The Devil's Dyke

On Dyke's high head I stand,

And looking west

O'er Cissbury showing clear against the sky

In crimson gold aflame,

I watch the setting sun.

The sea-breeze, laden with the scent

Of yellow gorse and fragrant thyme

Is nectar to my soul.

The tinkle of a sheep-bell far below

In Poynings, and the village church bell's chime

Mingle in sweet and mellow symphony.

A. E. F. (Sussex County Magazine, August, 1939)

Surely no more remote location has ever been chosen for a commercial pleasure gardens than the Devil's Dyke, that great hill which commands such superb views over the Sussex Weald. It has been said that on a clear day, Windsor Castle can be seen from here, but we leave that for readers to judge for themselves. What we can say is that the summit is more than 700 feet above sea level, and to the south overlooks the Channel from Beachy Head to Selsey Bill. To the north, Crowborough may be seen on the right and Hindhead on the left, with Leith Hill directly in front. What remains of the forests of Ashdown and Worth, Highbeech and St Leonard's, forms the skyline while smaller woods stretch their way to its lower slopes. The village of Poynings nestles almost immediately below. Newtimber and Wolstonbury Hills lie on the eastern flank, while in the opposite direction, Chanctonbury, with its mutilated crown of beech trees, towers over the western reaches of the county.

Gaze at the landscape spread out before you, and if not a Sussex man already, you surely become one at that moment. Then turn your head. A crowded car-park, a busy restaurant, chattering sightseers and the spell is broken. Yet however many people there are, the numbers are nothing to what they were. In its hey day over 100 years ago, more pleasure-seekers visited the Dyke than any other venue in the south. This was because a certain entrepreneur considered that the views – no matter how wonderful – were not sufficient to entice Brighton's holiday crowds. He felt that some additional form of attraction was required. So, with this in mind, various amusements and novelties of a fairground nature were installed. That they succeeded is beyond dispute. It is claimed, for instance, that towards the latter end of the 19th century, an astonishing 30,000 members of the public visited the site during the course of a single bank holiday. The promoter must have rubbed his hands with glee, and the fact that an influential and vocal minority deplored what was described as "the desecration of the Downs by Southern Cockneys" worried him not at all.

> This unfortunate spot cannot be avoided save on foot, for on horseback, the escarpment to the north is too steep to be followed; it is therefore best to take it boldly – unpleasant though it is.

Thus wrote Wilfrid Ball, author and artist, and the quotation is from his book *Sussex,* which was published in 1906.

A few years later, A. Hadrian Allcroft recorded the following acid comment in his topographical study entitled *Downland Pathways.*

"The place was," he said

> ...a mount of temptation with vulgarities that profane the spot, and a so-called hotel; which frets through an incongruous existence behind red, white and blue elephants 700 feet in the air.

Strong words indeed, but the sentiments expressed were shared by many others who hated the commercial exploitation, and feared that a tourist invasion would inflict lasting damage to the ancient site. They protested in vain, the venue had caught the public's imagination, and great crowds regularly visited the place. During the height of the season, the narrow white road crossing the hills was jammed with holiday traffic. People walked, people cycled, while horse-drawn conveyances of every description, gigs, barouches, coaches and wagonettes, all clattered along amidst clouds of dust as they made their cheerful way to the Dyke.

Perhaps nothing indicates the swift growing popularity of the resort more

An early print showing the western view from the Dyke

clearly than the decision to link it with the South Coast Railway. This was an engineering feat of some magnitude when bearing in mind the level to which the track had to rise. For the passengers however, it was but the first in a series of modern marvels. We say this because upon arriving at the destination, they were confronted with, of all things, an Aerial Cableway in which those who dared, could cross the Devil's Ditch. And if that was not enough, they could, having disembarked, descend gracefully to Poynings in a lift car operated by a Steep Grade Railway.

From 1897 onwards, it is probably correct to say that the Dyke as a tourist attraction had reached the high peak of its fame. By the end of the Edwardian era, its crowd-drawing capacity had begun to decline, but before examining why this should have occurred, let us go back to the beginning and trace if we can, the different stages that ultimately led to the site's pre-eminence as a Victorian pleasure ground.

The first thing to clearly establish, is the meaning of the name, the Devil's Dyke. It is believed to be Saxon in origin and refers not, as many suppose, to the deep ditch or chasm that cleaves its way through the hills at that point, but rather to a huge man-made bank of earth which runs approximately 200 yards east and west over the Downs, and in the process, cuts off the 40 acres which forms the top of Dyke Hill. This bank is all that remains of a neolithic hill fort, one of the largest in the county, and when the Saxons first set eyes on it, they were mightily impressed. It could not

8

have been raised by mere mortals they reasoned, it must be the work of the Devil. Therefore they called it the Devil's Dyke, or the Poor Man's Wall, which is a respectful Sussex euphemism for his Satanic Majesty's strenuous efforts.

References to the place may be found in early books on the district. For example, in *The Birds of Sussex* by William Borrer, which was published in 1891, the author, when describing Great Bustards (*Otis tarda*) informed the reader that "they were most numerous on a part of the Downs between the Dyke and a place known as Thunder's Barrow." He went on to say that the bird:

> …was often hunted with greyhounds by my grandfather, who died at an advanced age in 1844. He told me that he had had many a good course with these birds. He used to go out early in the morning, after a foggy night, to look for them feeding in the wet turnips, when they were so thoroughly soaked as to be unable to fly. He generally found them in

Another early print (about 1846) which features the first purpose-built inn to be erected at the Dyke

little parties of from five to ten, and sometimes took five or six in the morning, commonly young birds, though occasionally he had known an old one to be caught, but they avoided them as much as possible, as when overtaken by dogs, they fought savagely and had more than once damaged the greyhounds.

The Great Bustard has long since been hunted to extinction on the South Downs, so its presence in the area of the Dyke during the early 1800s, shows what an inaccessible spot it must still have been. The only practical approach was an extremely rough and ready track from the south. Yet despite the difficulties of the terrain, people had been making the journey for years, just to see the remarkable views. Even royalty has succumbed to its charms, for it is on record that William IV, together with Queen Adelaide frequently made the trip when residing at Brighton. By all accounts their excursions were spectacular safari-type affairs consisting of fifty carriages or more. The young Queen Victoria was also a noted frequenter of the district and is reported to have ridden there on horseback on several occasions.

One can be sure that where monarchs go, the populace will follow and being that it was 'the age of enterprise', few eyebrows were raised when around 1817, the first inn or place of refreshment opened for business on the famous hill. The premises, which could hardly have been considered an embellishment to an area of such outstanding beauty was, in the words of a local guide, nothing more than:

...a wooden hut which formerly stood on wheels near the top of Ship Street. One of its earliest landlords was Tommy King, a well-known fiddler.

Whether Mr King's ability was confined to the violin or otherwise was not made clear! But that he ran a successful establishment cannot be doubted. Indeed it prospered to such an extent that a few years later in 1831, the hut was demolished and a small inn was erected nearby.

The new premises were opened by a George Cheeseman, but his reign was short. Four years later, William Thacker became 'mine host' and remained so for fifty years. Under his astute proprietorship, the inn flourished so much, that in 1871 he built a substantial new hotel. The former building went the same way as the original hut. Thacker, with possibly one exception, did more to establish the popularity of the venue than any other landlord before or since. He realised an obvious truth early on, which was

that regular and reliable transportation from Brighton was a necessary inducement to tempt prospective customers.

He therefore subsidised carriages and later, wagonettes for this purpose, and his initiative combined with selective advertising did the trick. An example of some of the advance publicity the hotel received can be found in *Friend's Guide to Brighton*, an excellent little handbook that in those days was purchased by practically every visitor who came to the resort. In extolling the virtues of the Dyke, the publication described it as:

...the premier attraction immediately around Brighton, and may be visited without distress to the average pedestrian, or by means of wagonettes, which start from the King's Head, in West Street.

Mr Friend (who was well named as far as the landlord of the Dyke Hotel was concerned) went on to say:

From the Head of the Dyke, where the Dyke Hotel (a commodious and most comfortable hostelry, which Mr Thacker has conducted for about half a century) is situated, there is obtainable a magnificent panoramic view.

An illustration of a horse-drawn wagonnette (the type of which ran daily between Brighton and the Dyke) in front of Mr Thacker's new and altogether more commodious hotel

Undoubtedly helped by such warm recommendation, trade steadily increased, and the South Coast Railway Company, believing it to be a good business venture, linked up with the site by a single-track branch line. This opened in 1887 and ran from Dyke Halt Junction (later renamed Aldrington). It consisted of three and a half miles of continuously winding rising track, and became familiarly known as the 'zig-zag railway'.

Initially there was concern that the project might destroy the natural grandeur of the Dyke, but the imperturbable Mr Friend knew better. He informed his readers that:

> It will be a satisfaction to all lovers of this beautiful district to be assured that the Directors of the railway have given great attention to this matter, and it has been decided that the railway shall be constructed and the station placed in such a position as will not in any way interfere with the Dyke itself or its attractive surroundings.

That was precisely how it was done. Dyke Station was discreetly constructed on lower ground to the south and west of the hill top, and upon arrival, visitors were required to make their way up a fenced path to the road, and from there to walk a further 400 yards or so in order to reach the hotel. This enforced perambulation in no way detracted from the public's pleasure, people were becoming more conscious of the benefits of fresh air and exercise, as was illustrated by the remarks of a certain Alderman Davey at the inaugural meeting of the railway in 1883. Speaking glowingly about the attractions of the Dyke, he is reported to have claimed:

> "If a gentleman in London was suffering from ill-health and went for a stroll along the promenade and then paid a visit to the Dyke in the afternoon, it would do him more good than many a five-guinea fee paid to a physician."

How true, and those present shared his sentiments. Mr Thacker, who also attended, could not resist adding, that he had resided at the Dyke for more than 48 years, and thought that the fact of his being enabled to stand upon his legs and get about at the age of 73, should be in itself proof of the salubrity of the spot, and ample inducement for people to visit it.

The new line opened two years after Mr Thacker had retired from the proprietorship. From then on, apart from being closed for three years during the First World War, it ran without interruption until 1938, which was the date it ceased to operate. The last journey was an emotional affair. Almost 400 passengers squeezed aboard to be entertained by a band playing in the saloon coach. Fog signals were fired, and cheering crowds lined the track for most of the route.

Its closure prompted one lady to write to the *Sussex County Magazine*. Referring to her childhood on the Dyke Hills before 1914, she recalled:

> I have a very vivid picture of the 'fussy' little train which chugged past our house daily as we were sitting at meals with our father, Mr Holmes of Gibbett's Farm. I think that after it left the Dyke Halt, ours must have been the only house that it passed until reaching the Dyke. There was a steep ascent just as it passed the windows of our house, and during the summer months it was often so full that it almost came to a standstill, whilst in the winter it frequently had no passengers at all. Many a dark winter's evening by the aid of a lantern my sister and I would go across the meadow from our house, climb over the railway fence and over the line, to visit our friends who lived in the nursery on the other side, and excepting for Messrs Rookes, the stone masons, not another house was within sight. With the demolition of that little railway line was severed the last link of our old home, and although Holmes Avenue is named after my father, there is now no sign of the farm in which we lived.

Gibbett's Farm

The Dyke Railway station, a charming photograph showing a newly arrived group of day-trippers setting off for the resort

A slightly different view of the Dyke railway station, showing the nearby farmhouse, outbuildings and haystacks. There were no buffers to stop runaway trains here as the rising ground at the end of the line made such a precaution unnecessary. The curving path to the right of the picture led up to the main road and on to the Dyke.

14

The Aerial Cableway as seen from the road approaching the Dyke. The track passing close to the pylon is a bridle path that leads to Poynings.

Hubbard, it was erected in 1894, and costing sixpence for the return journey, proved to be very popular, even if many who used it, only did so to drop lumps of chalk in to gulch! For those interested in statistics, an official guide states:

> The full distance between the cable anchorages was 1200 feet (365.7m) with a clear central span of 650 feet (198.1m). An open cage served to carry eight passengers (other accounts suggest only four) the journey taking less than three minutes. An oil engine supplied the traction power.

During the previous year, 1893, a switchback or gravity railway had been added to the attractions. It was a short, simple, yet an effective device, consisting of an eighty-yard track that descended steeply from a raised platform into a deep hole. Passengers would plunge into the bowels of the earth, and then surge back up again.

Following Mr Thacker's retirement in 1885, Mr J. H. Hubbard, a wealthy big game hunter from British Columbia became the next landlord at the Dyke. He was the unnamed entrepreneur mentioned earlier in this history, and it was his business acumen, lively imagination and apparently bottomless pocket that transformed an already popular resort into the record breaking tourist attraction that it became.

Realising the importance of first impressions, Hubbard constructed two large pillars at the driveway entrance, each pillar being surmounted by a rather impressive model of an elephant. The surrounding area was kept neat and tidy, grass verges were clipped and shrubs were planted, the result being that the whole approach looked spick and span and extremely inviting. Yet despite such scrupulous attention, it is unlikely that the entrance would have been the first thing to catch the visitor's eye. That honour would surely be accorded to the Aerial Cableway, a remarkable structure, which dominating the eastern skyline, stretched between two pylons, one standing on either side of the chasm. Largely financed by Mr

The road entrance to the Dyke Hotel and grounds. The elephants mounted on the entrance pillars can be clearly seen, and the rather ramshackle structure to the right of the picture is in fact the starting point of the Gravity Railway.

Hubbard it would seem, was prepared to go to almost any expense to raise awareness of his establishment. In a newspaper article published in 1963, his granddaughter, Mrs G. Calcutt, described the place as being a sort of 'Grand Hotel'.

> In the Edwardian era, the premises bore no resemblance to the café there now. I have a photograph showing an ornate coffee room, complete with waiters, aspidistras, and a most enormous trolley. There is also a photograph of the staff – chefs, sous-chefs, stillroom men, grooms and boot boys.

According to a guide book, the coffee room mentioned by Mrs Calcutt, was capable of seating up to 275 persons. Other attractions included two bandstands, an observatory, and a camera obscura. In addition there were swingboats, a spiral slide, something described as a 'bicycle railway', and horses for riding.

An unusual view of the Aerial Cableway, showing the buildings at both ends. They not only housed the power components, but also served as departure and arrival points for the passengers.

Evidently a believer in the maxim that 'variety is the spice of life,' Mr Hubbard was constantly on the lookout for different novelties to claim the public's attention. Thus it transpired one Easter weekend that visitors to the site were confronted by a gigantic statue of Britannia, purchased apparently from a naval exhibition. On another occasion, a wooden model of a huge cannon was mounted in a prominent position overlooking the weald.

A wooden model of a 110-ton naval cannon

But what surely was the most unlikely item ever to be displayed on the Dyke hillside was a whale's skull. The head of the unfortunate mammal had been washed ashore near Brighton, and one of those who helped drag it up the beach was Mr Hubbard's son. In consequence it was transported to the pleasure ground and exhibited in front of the hotel. A plaque explained where it was found and when. This proved to be a controversial undertaking however, for although trippers were interested enough, conservationists and other critics of the landlord's brash business methods were predictably hostile. In his book, *Downland Pathways*, A. Hadrian Allcroft summed up the general feeling of distaste in the following terse lines:

> ...were this a hill in France, the people of that land would, one fancies, have reared upon it a Madonna, or at least a Calvary, and left the whale's bones to the decent sea.

Exposure to the elements at a high and open spot did what the protestors failed to do, for the bones deteriorated to such an extent that they were eventually dismantled and dumped at the side of the building. There they remained. Time passed, the proprietorship changed, staff came and went, and after a while, no one was left who knew the history of the remains.

Enquiries into the background of the bones were met by a shrug of the shoulder or a shake of the head. They became shrouded in mystery, but in fairness, such ignorance was hardly surprising, since whales are not usually to be found on top of the Downs.

A later view of the Dyke Hotel. This is the same building that Mr Thacker erected, but as can be seen, a first floor storey has been added to the western end. Horse-drawn wagonettes are pulled up in front of the premises, and to the right of the picture is a Tea Room cum Souvenir Shop with a verandahed front.

Another of Mr Hubbard's successful schemes was to allow a Romany fortune-teller by the name of Gipsy Lee, to operate from a tent or caravan that was pitched in a small grove of trees near to the hotel entrance. This lady was also known as the Queen of the Gypsies, and did a fine business at the resort – so fine as to permit her granddaughter to be educated at Elmhurst, a private boarding school for girls and young ladies which once stood in Station Road in nearby Burgess Hill. Daisy Upton, née Street, who was a pupil there at the same time, recalled that when the fortune-teller visited the premises to see the child, her demeanour and bearing was such that the headmistress and teachers treated her as if she really were a Queen!

In his book, *Highways and Byways in Sussex*, E.V. Lucas refers to this interesting woman:

> A change that is to be regretted is the exile to the unromantic neighbourhood of the Dyke Station of the Queen of Gypsies, a swarthy ringletted lady of peculiarly comfortable exterior who splendid (yet a little sinister) in a scarlet shawl and ponderous gold jewels, used once to emerge from a tent beside the Dyke Inn and allot husbands fair or dark. She was an astute reader of her fellows, with an eye too searching to be deceived by the removal of tell-tale rings. A lucky shot in respect to a future ducal husband of a young lady now a duchess, of the accuracy of which she was careful to remind you, increased her reputation tenfold in recent years. Her name is Lee, and of her title of Queen of the Gypsies there is, I believe, some justification.

Mr Lucas could well have added that it was not only the common throng who consulted Gypsy Lee. The fair and famous also sought her out; members of the English Royal Family, Indian Rajahs, Mr W. E. Gladstone, Mr Rothschild, Madame Patti and Lily Langtry to name but a few. She resided at the Dyke for over 30 years, and made many successful predictions, probably the best known being that King Edward V11 would not be crowned on the appointed day. We can only hope that she did not anticipate the sad circumstances of her own demise, which occurred at Haywards Heath Mental Hospital in 1911.

Another major venture instigated by landlord Hubbard, was the construction of a steep grade railway on the precipitous northern slope of Dyke Hill. According to an article by O. J. Morris that appeared in the *Locomotive*, it consisted of:

> ...a double track of 35 lb vignoles rail, laid on longitudinal baulks tied by cross transoms anchored to piles driven in the chalk.

When operating, two connected cars, each capable of carrying fourteen passengers, travelled at approximately three miles per hour in opposite directions, up and down, not one, but three differing gradients, the steepest of which was 1 in 1.5. Power was supplied from an oil engine situated in a building at the top, which also doubled as the station.

The Steep Grade Railway which descended to Poynings. The building at the top housed the power unit and also served as the station.

Following the railway's opening in 1897, a newspaper report in the *Brighton Gazette* stated:

> The cars do not move rapidly, but are kept well under control from first to last. They travel easily and smoothly and there is an utter absence of anything in the way of sensation. The journey is certainly a curious one, but that is all. Of course it is pleasant, the cars affording a charming view of the country, and there is the further attraction of the novelty of the whole thing.

A view from the foot of the Steep Grade Railway

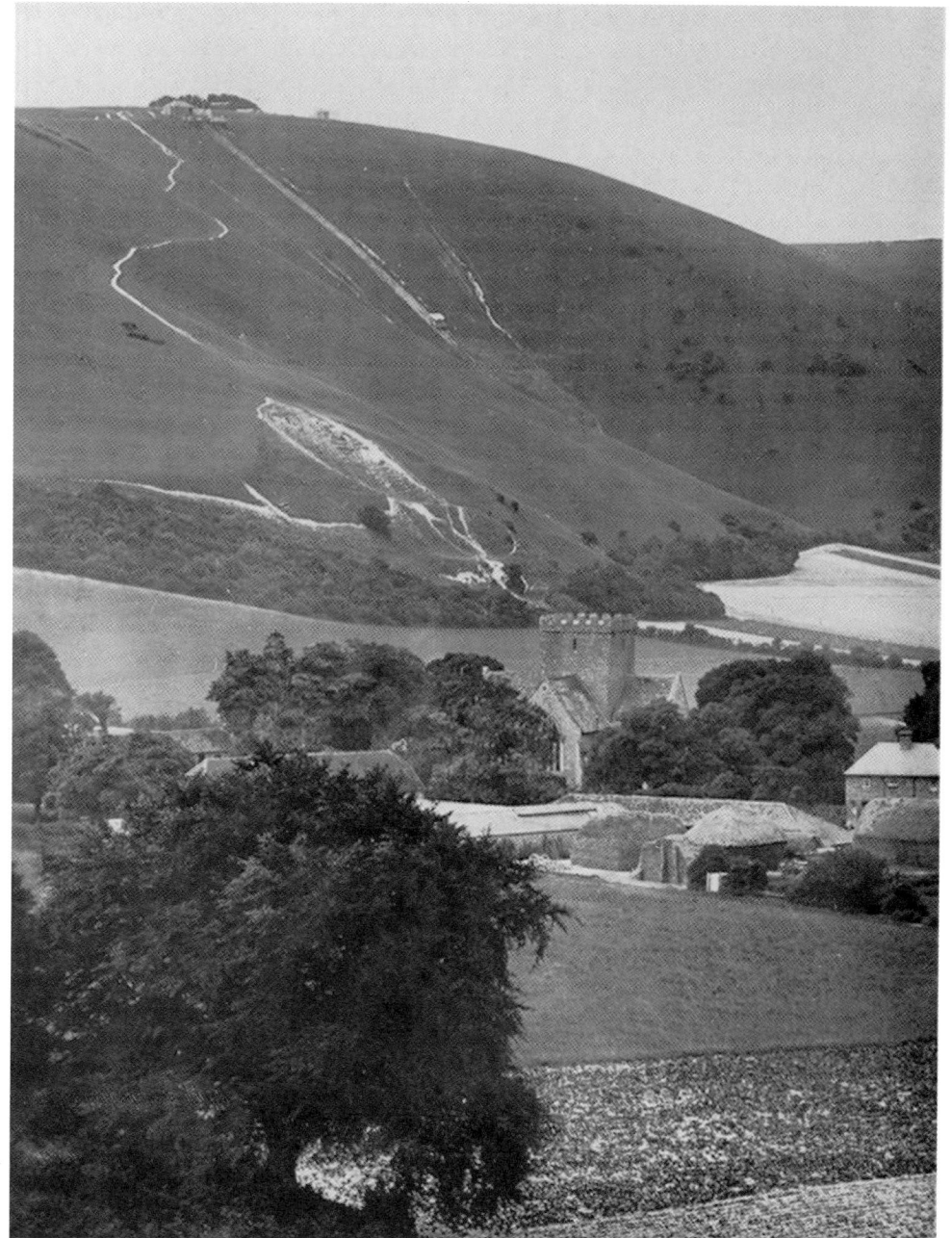

A distant view of the Dyke with Poynings Church in the foreground shows the Steep Grade Railway in action.

To Mr Hubbard's chagrin, his different transportation schemes failed to bring the financial return expected. Not because the public did not use the services provided, on the contrary, there was no shortage of paying passengers. The trouble was that they were not using them to go to his hotel. What he had done in effect, was to create a quick and easy route from the formerly remote community of Poynings, to the hustle and bustle of modern Brighton. Most travellers then, were either heading south to the seaside, or north, by-passing the Dyke Hotel on their way to other tea gardens that had sprung up in the near neighbourhood. Try as he might, this unexpected turn of affairs was a problem the landlord could never resolve, so in 1908, eleven years after its opening, the Steep Grade Railway together with the Aerial Cableway (two extremely successful engineering projects) ceased to function pending ultimate demolition.

Dennett's Corner – The photograph of this rather exposed little tea garden situated close to the railway station, perfectly illustrates the dilemma of the proprietor of the Dyke Hotel. The more he spent on his resort, the more people came, but instead of profiting from his investments, all he saw was potential customers being diverted by establishments such as this. Whether the unsteady-looking screen (centre left) served as a windbreak, an advertising hoarding, or had been erected to provide the diners with a modicum of privacy, we cannot say.

The closing of these services coincided with Mr Hubbard's own departure from the resort. This dynamic showman who in a relatively short period had updated and transformed the amenities at the famous Sussex hill top, finally retired and returned to his home in Canada. His leaving was well timed, for the world of the 20th century was a swiftly changing place. Venues like his suddenly found themselves subjected to pressure from newer forms of entertainment, such as the fledgling cinema industry. In consequence, business at the Dyke faltered and declined. That is evident from photographs of the period, which reveal unkempt grass verges, unrepaired fencing, and roof-tops plastered in advertising hoardings.

The property changed hands several times during the next few years, without enjoying any noticeable upturn in its fortunes. Then, in the early 1920s, it came into the possession of Mrs Maud Barrassford who was the widow of the lessee of the Brighton Hippodrome. She sought to popularise both places by organising a series of Saturday afternoon marathon races from the Court Theatre in New Road to the Devil's Dyke. These had a limited success only, and it must be said that the lady's professed fondness for the site cooled considerably when she failed to gain planning permission to erect a small estate of bungalows on land adjacent to the hotel. The refusal, much as it pleased the 'protectionists', did not allay their concern. Sooner or later they feared, someone would succeed where she had failed. Therefore it must have been a considerable relief to her opponents when in 1928, a great benefactor to Brighton and the surrounding district, the wealthy Sir Edward Carden, bought the freehold for £9,000, and then re-sold it for the same amount to the Corporation. This gesture was made on the understanding that the body in question would do their utmost to protect the site from any future spoilation. As if to confirm this, on the 30th May the same year, the Duke of York paid an official visit to the Dyke Estate, and after bestowing his royal seal of approval, dedicated it to "the use of the public forever."

In 1945, the hotel, having survived two world wars, was gutted by fire. Ten years were to pass before it was replaced with another building. In a further ten years that too had gone, and the present establishment, the first (according to a guide book) to be built with local materials, was erected in its place.

To conclude; in 1964, Mr Kramer, the then proprietor, proposed that the water-tanks of the hotel, which he considered unsightly, should be disguised by a full size replica of a windmill. Furthermore, he stated that it would add interest to the resort if there were a new attraction. With regards to this, he suggested that a scale model of the 'Temple of Abu Simbel' in Egypt, be built into the side of the chasm! Despite the fact that such a novel idea flew in the face of Sir Herbert Carden's intentions, consideration was given to it, but the negotiations and conditions proved to be so protracted and difficult, that the promotor eventually lost interest. A good thing too. However, it must be admitted that there was a certain 'grand folly' about the scheme, and if it did nothing else, Mr Kramer's imaginative idea showed that the entrepreneurial spirit of the old Dyke landlords, still lived on.

Gipsy Lee – the Fortune Teller at the Devil's Dyke

The 'Haunted Lake' at the Devil's Dyke may be found at the foot of the South Downs at Poynings, although because of the drop in water levels, it is not much more than a pond now. As such it is all that remains to remind people that water gushing out of local springs was at one time sufficient to operate two watermills in the area.
The site is believed to be haunted by the spirits of three village boys, who back in 1883, were swimming there. The story goes that two of them got out of their depth and called for help. The third lad ran to the church where the congregation had just arrived for Evening Service, but he was so overcome with fear that he could not make himself understood. Returning to the lake, he saw the last struggles of his friends, a sight which so upset him that he died later of grief.

The Promenade Grove

According to our researches, it was in 1793 or thereabouts that the first Pleasure Gardens in Sussex were opened at Brighton. Called the Promenade Grove (an apt name) they provided the most congenial surroundings for 'fashionables' to gather, to observe, and more importantly, to be observed! Ladies and gentlemen would congregate within the grounds to gossip and partake of light refreshments while a military band played for their amusement. Should inclement weather spoil the proceedings, then the company retired to what was described as an "elegant saloon" where they could continue to exchange news, sip beverages, or perhaps acquaint themselves with all that was of interest in the latest journals. And as pleasant as this light-hearted intercourse must have been, it was a mere prelude to the delights that followed, for it was after sunset that the Grove really came to life. As the shadows lengthened, countless coloured lights flickered amongst the trees, whilst garlands of flowers decorated the walks and scented an evening air, already resonant with the melodies of orchestra and minstrels. In a very short time indeed the venue became a popular rendezvous, an oasis of culture and most definitely the place to be seen. Society Lions, who previously had only the treeless Steine as a platform to parade their charms, were irresistibly drawn by the siren voices and twinkling illuminations of the new and infinitely more interesting stage just across the road.

But there was no pleasing everyone, and although few in number, some critics of the venture did exist, as is revealed by the tone of a contemporary article published in the *New Brighton Guide*. The author, Anthony Pasquin, sourly declared:

> At the lower end of North Street is a sort of Vauxhall, called the Promenade Grove; it is a small enclosure of a paddock, tormented from its native simplicity, befringed with a few gawky poplars [Pasquin was wrong, they were elms] and decorated with flowers, bowers, benches, frogs, ground ivy, a ditch and a wooden box for the minstrels.

Pasquin it would seem was the type of journalist who would as soon dip his pen in vitriol as ink. Not much escaped his notice, and many respectable citizens were pilloried as result. However, a fairer description may be discovered in a book entitled, *Brighton in the Olden Time*. The author, John George Bishop, had this to say:

> The grounds of the Grove were tastefully, though not profusely, laid out with choice flowering and other shrubs. But its chief attractions were the avenues of noble elms; for, in addition to those now forming "The Rookery", there appears to have been a parallel double-row lower down, running straight across the centre of the present lawn from north to south, and known, we believe, as "The Rutland Walk"...

> ...Once within its gates, the town, and all associated with it, was almost lost to view. The only side open to peering eyes from without was the East, from the present road through the Pavilion Grounds (then known as East Street) but even here, along its extent, there was an enclosed meadow, with doubtless a hedgerow. The green sward of the Grove was as soft and velvety as the pile of a Turkey carpet, and always kept nicely mown and smooth; the ground, too, was perfectly level, the undulations of the present western lawn of the Pavilion Grounds being an after-formation. Some portion of the Grove was originally a farm meadow known as the "Dairy Field", and it extended (from north to south) almost from the Spring Walks (now Church Street) to Prince's Place, and included the ground now covered by the western portion of the Pavilion Dormitories. On the west, the Grove was bounded by an enclosed meadow belonging to the Society of Friends, and known as, "The Quakers Croft", through a part of which the new road was subsequently formed.

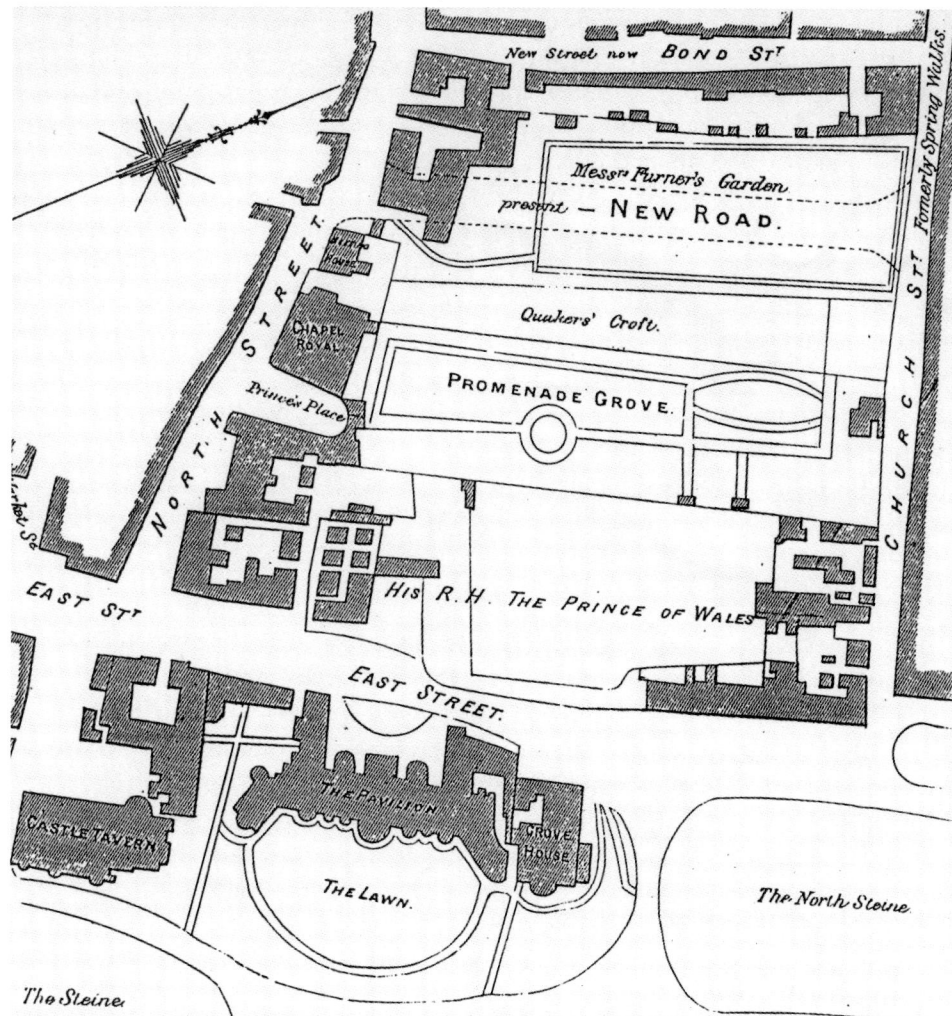

An 1803 map showing the position of the Promenade Grove in relation to the proposed 'New Road' (which compensated for the cutting short of East Street as a public road) and North Street, Church Street, as well as the original Marine Pavilion.

The Grove was open every day during the season (Sunday evenings excepted) and operated on a subscription basis, each member paying half a guinea for the use of the facilities. Non-members were charged one shilling for the day, but would only be admitted if introduced by a subscriber. Whether the enterprise was the creation of a company, or the scheme of an individual entrepreneur is not exactly certain, although we are inclined to think the latter, as the final paragraph of the original prospectus states:

> Mr Bailey, under whose sole direction and management the Promenade Grove will be opened, humbly hopes the plans and terms which he has thus the honour of procuring, will meet the encouraging approbation of a generous and discerning public. He most sincerely assures them that his endeavours to deserve success shall be unabating; his care to exclude improper company most particular; and his attention to give general satisfaction, unremitting.

What precisely was deemed to be improper company was not specified, which was perhaps wise, for the establishment basked in the warm glow of patronage cast by The Prince of Wales, and his somewhat raffish companions. This came about because he, despite being heir to the throne and the so-called first gentleman of Europe, had an insatiable weakness for life's pleasures, and where better to indulge himself than at his palace by the sea? Not surprisingly, the Bohemian atmosphere of the nearby Gardens appealed to him. Indeed, his enjoyment of the venue was so great, that he declared he would give it his royal support. This was amply demonstrated when he and four hundred guests were present at one of the grandest Public Breakfasts of the opening season. It was, according to a report of the time:

> ...most elegantly attended by all that is noble, fashionable, or respectable at Brighton. There has rarely been such an assembly of beauty and fashion, who all expressed their approbation of this novel species of entertainment, and seemed unwilling to quit the enchanting place, and many staid till near four o'clock.

With the Prince as its patron, the Grove remained in high favour, and so it is hardly surprising that on his birthday during the second season (1794) the management celebrated the event by holding a grand evening festival in the grounds. Over 1,200 guests strolled through the brilliantly illuminated gardens, several bands played martial airs, while the saloon and other buildings were tastefully ornamented with festoons and musical devices in various reflecting lamps. Along the Rutland Walk was a transparent painting of His Royal Highness's coronet and crest, adorned with red roses, and the words, 'Long Live the Prince.' At the end of the Cross Walk was the Garter Star, decorated with woodbines and lilies; and displayed on the lawn were His Royal Highness's initials, beautifully fashioned in flowers and crowned with a wreath of laurel; the whole encircled with the British Oak and acorns, and the motto, 'Brighton's support.'

The 1795 season was an auspicious one for the Grove, for the Prince and his newly-wedded wife, Princess Caroline of Brunswick were residing in Brighton at the time. And so in appreciation of the Royal patronage that continued to be bestowed upon the gardens, special amusements were announced in honour of the Prince's birthday. These in addition to the usual illuminations and concerts, included for the first time as far as we are aware, what was described as, "a grand display of fireworks". Indeed, the exhibition was called, "truly magnificent", and in *Brighton in the Olden Times,* there is a detailed account of what took place. The author, Mr Bishop, wrote:

> There was a second display on September 22nd, at which over 1000 spectators were present; and it exceeded in a variety of fanciful design and splendour of exhibition all previous efforts. The last piece of the display was a graceful tribute to Princess Caroline, and consisted of – Three Pedestals, supporting the initials of H.R.H the Princess of Wales, in Slow Fire; a Grand Reprize of Nine Fans, or Chinese Fire, with a discharge of Maroons; to conclude with two Bombshells Illuminated, and a Flight of Rockets.

The imagination of the promoters seems to have known no bounds. In the next season for instance (1796) the main event was advertised as the "Original Poney Races", which were to be staged in the Amphitheatre of the Grove. Starting at the unusual hour of 8.30pm, the actual racing consisted of three heats and a final, with an orchestra playing during the intervals. The track was lit in various devices with different coloured lamps and nearly 600 spectators enjoyed the fun. The evening was considered to be such a success, that it was repeated on many occasions.

In 1797, "Public Tea Drinking with Music" was all the rage, while the popularity of the evening concerts had grown to such an extent that they were attracting top of the bill artistes from Drury Lane and Covent Garden.

Later on, a quite different form of entertainment was provided for the clientelle. Known as "The Fantoccini", it was, according to Mr Bishop, "a decided novelty". Unfortunately it has also proved to be somewhat of a mystery, for he did not explain precisely what was meant by the expression. A quote from an original announcement was included, but threw little light on the matter, stating merely that it was:

> A musical Entertainment entitled "Les Trois Recettes," to which will be added the favourite petite piece of "L'Erreur Du Moment," with Dancing and other Entertainments between the Acts.

"Les Trois Recettes" means "The Three Recipes" (or possibly, "The Three Returns") while "L'Erreur Du Moment" translates as "Mistake of the Moment." The word *Fantoccini* we believe to be the plural of Fantoccio, which is Italian for puppet. So from this we deduce that the patrons of the Grove were probably watching, and by all accounts enjoying, some sort of puppet or marionette theatre set to music.

But puppets and ponies apart, the staple fare of the Grove always remained concerts and fireworks. As Mr Bishop said:

> It were needless to detail the amusements of the Grove during the next season or two; there were breakfasts and concerts, and concerts and breakfasts; fireworks and illuminations; illuminations and fireworks...

All of this was not least because the Prince of Wales was exceedingly fond of both – especially the fireworks. To give some indication of his passion for the subject, he appointed a certain Signor Hengler as "Artist and Engineer in Fireworks to H.R.H. the Prince of Wales and the Duke of Clarence" (evidently another devotee). Despite such an extraordinary title, the Signor appears to have been a worthy choice indeed, his skill must have been considerable if judged by the description of two pieces he put on for his patron:

(1) A Representation of Two Ships in Action at Sea. The same as was performed in honour of Lord Viscount Duncan at Hampton Court, where the Royal Family were present, and other persons of distinction, with a beautiful transparency of 'Rule Britannia' in a glory of brilliant fire.

(2) A superb piece of mechanism, soley invented and executed by Signor Hengler, representing 'Two Rattle Snakes in Pursuit of a Butterfly' whose beautiful colours will be represented by blue, yellow, green, and other diversified fireworks; at the same time, two splendid Mosaicks will be set on fire by a flying pidgeon.

In 1801, Chinese fireworks were introduced for the first time in Brighton. They were described as being infinitely superior to those previously used, and this view was more than confirmed by the subscribers who gathered to watch a stupendous representation of Halley's Comet. Sadly though, few opportunities remained to see them, for it was suddenly announced that the Prince of Wales, who had been the Lessee of the neighbouring Dairy Field since 1795, had purchased the Grove with the intention of closing it to the public, and converting part of the grounds to a Tennis Court. 1802 it transpired, was to be the final season.

Bitter as the decision must have been, it is a measure of the Proprietor's character that the dismay he assuredly felt, was not permitted to cloud the festivities. As Mr Bishop (misquoting the Bard) was to later observe:

"Nothing became him like the leaving it" – Not only did he do his best to make a pleasant ending, but he availed himself of the opportunity to prove his appreciation of the patronage bestowed upon him during his career.

So the show went on, bright, breezy, and as inventive as ever, until September 9th, which was the date when the last Grand Gala was staged. Entitled, "A Day at Brighton," it was a truly splendid production which included the celebrated Tight Rope Artiste, Signor Saxoni. This performer, having recently returned from a triumphant tour of Paris, delighted the crowd by executing a Tambourine Dance, the Hornpipe, the Russian Manual, and other intricate and daring exercises – all while balanced on the rope. The entertainment then drew to a close with a scintillating display of fireworks, the principal part being, "The Awesome Spectacle of Mount Vesuvius after an Eruption".

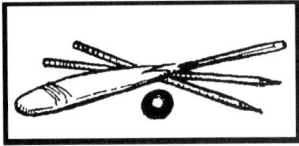

Ireland's Royal Pleasure Gardens

Townsfolk who were anxious to preserve the traditions of the Promenade Grove, attempted to do so at other tea gardens that had sprung up along the Marine Parade. Unfortunately their efforts were all in vain, the establishments hardly compared with their illustrious predecessor, and so not surprisingly, failed to catch on. In fact, twenty years were to pass before a similar venue was opened in the general vicinity, and by coincidence, this, like the Promenade Grove, was also associated with the Prince of Wales. Apparently he was, or had been, a keen cricketer, but by 1822, increasing age and a spreading waist-line, caused him to announce that his playing days were over. The pitch used by H.R.H. (reputed to be the finest in the country at the time) was situated at the northern end of the Level, on land owned by a Mr Thomas Read Kemp, and he, following the Prince's retirement, donated a plot adjoining the southern edge of the cricket field to the local authority, on condition that it would be kept as an open space for ever. At the same time he sold ten acres on the northern boundary (where Park Crescent now stands) to a Mr James Ireland.

This gentleman had various and diverse interests in the town. For instance, he owned a Woollen Drapers establishment in North Street, and just a few doors away, an Undertaker's Parlour, both of which he was eventually to sell to the Hannington family. It would seem however that his greatest ambition was to be the Proprietor of a Pleasure Gardens, and it was almost certainly this idea that he had in mind when purchasing the land by the Level. He spent freely on the project, and the taste and imagination vested in its design is clearly revealed in an original print of the period, while the best written description that we could discover, was contained in an early publication entitled, *Sickelmores Select Views of Brighton,* which described the venue as follows:

> These delightful grounds, designated immediately by His Majesty, "The Royal Brighton Gardens", are entirely surrounded by a neat brick and flint wall, surmounted by a handsome chevaux de frize fence and roller. Two handsome lodges conduct to the cricket ground, the best, perhaps, in the country, the one at its south-west angle, and the other eastward. Near the former is a spacious bowling green, with raised banks, and a capital billiard-room and table. By the eastern lodge is the Hanover Arms Inn, with extensive stabling – but the latter is desirably obscured from the cricket ground, by a racket and five's court, a raised shrubbery, druidical seats etc. Centrally, on the north side is the grand promenade saloon, 60 feet by 40 feet, opening to an interesting view of the Level etc. Southward; and to the north, an indescribably fascinating prospect of the diversified attractions of the adjoining gardens. Beneath this saloon, on the ground floor, are various parlours or sitting rooms, reading rooms, a well constructed bar, with other tavern requisites, upon the best scale of comfortable accommodation. On the left as you enter the gardens, is a grotto, and on the right, a well stocked aviary, prettily designed, and of more than common dimensions. Advancing, you reach a sunken ground plot, with skirting seats, intended for bowls or dancing, approximating to which, within a space or two, is a semblance of an abbey, in Gothic style, with various compartments, containing seats and tables, and filling a site of about 40 feet by 30 feet. Passing through the abbey, by a wide straight vista, you traverse the entire centre of the place, reaching, at its extremity, a bridge which crosses a small canal to a Gothic castle. Beyond this is a Maze, the intricacies of which are ingeniously contrived; it is an improvement upon those at Hampton Court, and in the Sidney Gardens, at Bath, in the centre of which is a Merlin's Swing, of safe and elegant construction.

Ireland's Royal Brighton Gardens – The wide track curving up the hill is now Elm Grove at its junction with Lewes Road, and the large central pavilion stands approximately where a present day pedestrian might stroll around Park Crescent Terrace and Park Crescent Road.

Quite inexplicably, the Gardens turned out to be a resounding flop. They were in a good position, attractively laid out, and as we have gathered, contained many fascinating and novel features – but the public stayed away. Why, who can tell?

In an attempt to turn the business round, Ireland continued to pour money into the enterprise. He organised a balloon ascent, held frequent firework displays, staged grand concerts, and ran a poster campaign advertising a forthcoming "Demonstration of Flying". This particular attraction did succeed in drawing a crowd, but they were kept waiting too long, and consequently were out of humour by the time a performer, with wheels and pulleys strapped to his back, glided down a cable stretched between a building and the rustic bridge. To add to the somewhat farcical nature of the proceedings, the artiste, wearing flesh coloured tights was adorned with gossamer wings, and waved a flag in either hand as he made his descent. This proved too much for an audience that expected more for its money than a theatrical fairy, and the core of the membership broke ranks with the intention of scragging the poor man. He, with commendable swiftness, made good his escape through the maze.

Ireland's Royal Grounds

With creditors pressing hard, Mr Ireland must have fervently wished that he could vanish as easily, but fortune it seemed had deserted him. After losing all of his investment, he sold up and turned instead to the safer business of inn-keeping, becoming at one and the same time "Mine Host" at the nearby Hanover Arms, and the Golden Cross Inn, at Prince's Street. Later he was to hold the licence at the Kerrison Arms in Hove.

Doomed to commercial failure, the Gardens passed through many hands, deteriorating all the while. Mr Pierpoint, then Mr Brown, followed by Messrs Harvey and Box, all tried – and all failed. Inexplicably, the people did not? would not? come, so the venue closed in 1829.

Ginnett's Circus occupied the site for a while after this, however, the refusal of Brighton's magistrates to grant a drinking licence, caused the proprietor to move his business elsewhere.

A menagerie was also introduced at some point, but predictably lasted for only a matter of months.

It is a sad story, in six short years, the Royal Gardens, originally conceived as a 'prince's playground', were reduced to a refuge for vandals and vermin. The flower-beds became infested with weeds, the lawns grew rank, and the place, according to Clifford Musgrave, in his book, *Life in Brighton,* was:

...given over to travelling shows and fairs of the lowest description.

The Swiss Gardens

"...Ah, she must have gone to the Gardens... those Gardens... Dancing Hall, Theatre, sorcerers – every blessed thing..."

(Reference to the Swiss Gardens taken from George Moore's novel, Esther Waters*)*

They say that 'hope springs eternal,' but whether the old adage would have been applied to Mr James Britton Balley, a wealthy ship-builder from Shoreham, we are not entirely certain. Perhaps the invigorating quality of the sea air accounted for the gentleman's optimism? Whatever the cause, he was probably the only man on the southern coast (following Mr Ireland's ill-fated venture) who still had any faith in the commercial future of pleasure gardens. Yet in 1838, the year that the young Queen Victoria ascended to the throne, he opened such an establishment in his home-town by the sea, and called it 'The Swiss Gardens.' The resort, according to Henry Cheal, in *The Story of Shoreham,* contained many delightful attractions, including:

> ...bowls and archery, a well appointed theatre, a refreshment room for 1000 persons, a "magic cave" and an ornamental lake. The ball-room being possibly the finest in Sussex.[sic]

In those days, the railway track linking Brighton with Shoreham was still not completed, although work was proceeding apace. Also, it was no secret that the London, Brighton and South Coast Railway Company's plans were that once the service was operating, the time spent travelling between the two towns should not exceed eleven and a half minutes. So if he were in need of encouragement, such knowledge surely increased Mr Balley's resolve to persevere with his project, for he must have known that train travel, still very much a novel experience, would place his venue within easy reach of Brighton's considerable population, thereby ensuring a handsome return on his investment. If this was his reasoning, then he was absolutely right, for on 11th May, 1840, which was the day after the official opening of the line, 1, 750 passengers were carried to Shoreham, many of whom undoubtedly paid a visit to the Swiss Gardens, where in celebration of the event, the proprietor staged a Grand Fete.

The new resort was successful from the outset. People not only came from nearby towns and villages, but from as far afield as London and Portsmouth. Initially they came by coach or wagonette – or walked. Later (as we have said) they came by train, but most importantly – they came, and in vast numbers, often more than 5,000 visitors a day, which exceeded the local population by about two to one!

R. Sickelmore, the publisher to whom we referred earlier when dealing with Ireland's Royal Gardens at Brighton, also produced a delightful little visitor's guide, entitled, *A Rail-Road Trip to Shoreham, and a Visit to the Swiss Gardens.* There is no publication date, but examination of the contents reveal that it was printed during Mr Balley's reign, which means that the booklet would have appeared before 1860. This can be stated with reasonable confidence, because according to Roy Sharp, in Issue 22, *Sussex Industrial History:*

> Some years before his death in 1863, J. B. Balley sold the Gardens to a Mr Edward Goodchild.

The Guide which was probably commissioned by the Railway Company and the Garden's Proprietor, contains the most entertaining and informative descriptions of the venue, while the old-fashioned prose conjures up a world and way of life that has vanished for ever. For these reasons, and to also provide the reader with an opportunity of studying an original account of the time, we reproduce part of it here:

> On entering the garden by the principal gate, the eye is agreeably surprised by a view of the lake, its sedgy banks, skirted by graceful foliage, and studded with picturesque buildings, and its surface skimmed by a gay flotilla of pleasure boats, manned by merry adventurers, on voyages of discovery amidst its tiny rocks, and pretty islands.
>
> These little craft are well constructed, and perfectly safe, so that the most timid navigator need fear no worst accident than a sprinkle from the oar of some amateur waterman, who, in his laudable endeavours to go a-head, has unwittingly "caught a crab", or finding himself comfortably aground under the little fountain in the middle of the lake, which trifling casualties, although they 'moisten' the garments, seldom 'damp' the mirth of the parties; and it would seem, from the fresh bursts of laughter which invariably follow accidents of this sort, that cold water, judiciously applied,

outwardly, is an excellent stimulant to the visible faculties, and a good remedy in cases of hypochondria.

Those of our friends however, who have no desire to perform their ablutions in this manner, are recommended to make a tour of the lake in the "Basilisk", an elegant little steamer of half a horse power, which will contain eight to ten persons, and starts from the quay every ten minutes. The crew, consisting of 'one man,' will be found steady and attentive, and we have no hesitation in saying, that those who take a trip in this miniature ship, will be tempted to do so again before leaving the gardens.

But our friends are no doubt anxious to see the interior of the cottage, whose thatched roof, picturesque gables and chimneys, terminate the prospect from this point, so, if they will follow me through the little wicket gate to the right, we will stroll along the bank of the lake, and merely notice in passing, the Aviary, and a long building adjoining it, containing amongst other apartments, the reading room, where may be seen the prints of the day, and two pretty little rooms, fitted up for the games of bagatelle, and Chinese billiards. Passing by the directors office, and that very necessary appendage to the gardens, the kitchen, we must stop a moment, to look at a beautiful grotto, formed of moss, and covered by honey suckles and other odoriferous climbers, which are prettily trained over the rustic wood-work which decorates the exterior; there is a chalybeate spring inside, of whose virtues we can say nothing, having never had the curiosity to taste it, but being 'freshly prepared' every morning, we have no doubt of its excellence.

A line of pleasant arbours joins the grotto, and continues to the end of the lake, where, by a sudden turn to the left, we stand under the beautiful porch, formed by the projecting eaves of the cottage, whence we have another, and better general view of the lake. At the further end of the porch is a commodious lavatory, for the use of gentlemen, and facing it a conservatory, with a small fountain, of elegant design, playing in the midst. A placard, in a curiously made frame, announces that visitors of our sex are not permitted to pass 'through' the conservatory, as it leads to an apartment expressly set aside for the ladies. The furniture and decorations are in the same style as the other parts of the cottage, but arranged and

finished with perhaps more taste. It contains a small but select library, and globes; scrap books, albums and chess boards are placed on the different tables; in fact everything has been done to make this elegant little boudoir worthy of its fair occupants.

We will now step out of the door of the conservatory, and enter the ball room, the great door of which is in the centre of the cottage and facing the lake. The interior arrangement of this unique saloon, must strike everyone who beholds it for the first time, with sensations of pleasurable surprise; it is spacious and lofty, measuring 120 feet in length, by 45 feet in width, with a pitch of 25 feet; a peculiarly elegant gallery runs round three sides of the room, at one end of which is a stage for theatrical representations, concerts, etc., the necessary scenery and properties are on the spot, and can be ready for use at the shortest notice. The view of the room looking from the stage is quite fairy-like, and it is not until the spectator has examined its decorations in detail, that he can imagine so rich an effect could be produced by the use of such simple materials, as crooked twigs, rough bark, knots of pine, and fir apples, such is the case however, and with these, Mr Balley has contrived to rival the work of the most skilled carver. A daily exhibition of Phantasmagoria takes place here, and when the day closes, the younger visitors generally conclude the amusements with a dance, musical instruments being provided for the purpose.

After leaving the ball room and crossing over a bridge of steps, we find ourselves in the north garden, tastefully laid out in parterres of flowers, and studded with beautiful little summer houses. The observatory, which towers above our heads, is 60 feet in height, and the prospect from the top, will amply repay us for the trouble of mounting: here we have a complete view of the gardens, lake and archery grounds.

The little circular roof upon which we look down, is that of the Temple of the Oracle, to which we will descend. Its low door covered by mystical characters, opens at the slightest tap by invisible hands, we enter, and it closes in the same silent and mysterious manner; a narrow winding passage brings us at length into a chamber. Some amusing answers are made to the questions put to the oracle, and by the blushing cheeks of some of

Early print (circa 1840) entitled, 'View from the castle of Falkenstein'.

the fair querists, it would appear that they attach rather more importance to them than they would like to confess.

To the left, on going out of the temple, we pass under an arch overgrown with climbing plants, into the bowling green, archery and cricket ground. Here are bats, traps, bowls, ninepins, skittles, strewed on the ground at the service of anyone who chooses to pick them up, whilst bows, arrows, and all the necessary apparatus for those who like to exercise themselves, may be hired at a trifling cost.

The western side of the ground is flanked by a row of neat and shady arbours, where those who are content to remain as spectators, may repose in safety. Any attempt to dislodge them on the part of the crowd of visitors who are now pouring in at the gate opposite, is defended by a battery of six carronades, planted there doubtless for that express purpose. By the "right merry faces" approaching, however, I do not think there is much to be feared on that score.

I shall leave my friends to rest themselves after their walk. I must however inform them, that if they stand in need of refreshments, they will, by retracing their steps as far as the cottage, find a delightful little room, where they can be served with what they require, with as much privacy and comfort as in their own parlour.

Having conducted you into this comfortable retreat, your guide takes his leave. Farewell, and may the remembrance of to-day's ramble induce you to make a series of excursions to Shoreham and the Swiss Gardens.

The anonymous author paints a charming picture of the resort, making it easy to see why it became and remained, such a popular spot. There were two lakes linked by a narrow strait that was spanned by the "bridge of steps", referred to in the Guide. A place – if we may be forgiven a momentary diversion – which reminds us of a story told by an old Shoreham resident:

In the 1920s – he said – long after the gardens had closed, the landlord could still earn a few shillings by hiring out boats at so much an hour. Sometimes, when boys were on board, they'd not bother to return at the end of the session, and the more the landlord called out, the less likely they were to come. They'd just paddle around in the middle of the lake and cheek him. Well, the way of dealing with a situation like that was extremely simple. My father, who worked there at the time, stood all innocent like on the bridge, as if he was feeding the ducks or something, then, when the lads rowed underneath, he would suddenly jump in amongst them. I would have liked to see their faces. Pa said there was a right old tussle on occasion – but it did the trick.

Returning to more civilised times, it would appear that the price of admission covered not only entrance to the venue, but the use of many of the attractions within. There was for instance, free entry to an aviary containing rare and exotic birds collected from all over the world. Fishing for the huge carp that reputedly lurked in the depths of the lake, cost not a penny. Neither for that matter did access to the various mazes, arbours, greenhouses and playgrounds that could be discovered at every twist and turn along the way. As stated in the Guide, equipment such as ninepins and skittles etc was scattered about for the benefit of anyone who cared to use it. In addition, there were roundabouts, see-saws, swings and slides, as well as a host of similar contrivances, all designed to appeal to visiting holidaymakers, young or old.

Other entertainments included a good class cricket pitch, tennis courts, and facilities for skating during the winter months. Not everything was free however. At one time, a plaque erected outside the premises, stated:

No charge is made for any of the amusements in the Gardens – except a small one for; Billiards, Rifle Shooting and American Bowls.

We notice that neither archery or boating was included on this list, but rather suspect that they should have been. With regards to the latter, it is worth noting that as well as the paddle-steamer, there was a virtual fleet of vessels on the lakes – canoes, kayaks, dinghies, and many more besides. They were tremendously popular with the patrons, and it is hard to believe that someone as astute as Mr Balley, would have neglected such an obvious source of revenue.

Functions of one sort or another, occurred regularly at the Swiss Gardens. A band was usually in attendance, and it was said that the dazzling uniforms worn by the instrumentalists were only outshone by the gaudy feathers of some resident peacocks. These birds had the complete freedom

Lake and Temple Swiss Gardens Shoreham

of the resort, and strutted about the grounds like veritable 'Princes of the Orient'. By all accounts they were quite eye-catching, especially when set against the background of 'Gog' and 'Magog', two large and sinister effigies, whose purpose was to guard the entrance of the grotto (or "magic cave") that contained the chalybeate spring.

The carronades mentioned in the Guide were short barrelled, large-calibre ship's guns that were occasionally fired to herald an important event – or to liven up the customers! They discharged 'blank' shot of course, and therefore posed no threat to life or limb, or the nearby premises that fell within their range. Amongst these buildings were some pavilions (or

rooms) where entertainments known as Dioramas, Cosmoramas, and Panoramas could be viewed. A diorama, according to the *Oxford English Dictionary*, can be either:

> 1 – A spectacular painting (usually viewed through an aperture with sides continued towards the picture) in which, by changes in colour and direction of light thrown on or through it, atmospheric effects of various kinds are produced.
>
> 2 – A small scale representation of a scene with objects etc, in front of a painted background, viewed through an aperture from the front.

A panorama is a series of pictures forming an unbroken view of a surrounding region, arranged on the inside of cylindrical surface. The wall within a circular room would suit such a purpose nicely, always providing that the audience could be contained in the centre.

Quite what a cosmorama was, we are not too sure, but suspect that it might have been some sort of Magic Lantern presentation?

Another puzzling aspect of the resort was "The Castle of Falkenstein". It is mentioned time and again. In Issue 22, *Sussex Industrial History,* the author says that the name refers to a series of scenes presented by Mr George Ruff, a local artist, in the Diorama Pavilion. But rather confusingly, the same publication also contains an early engraving of the Swiss Gardens, entitled, "View from the Castle of Falkenstein" which tends to suggest that the castle was a building within the grounds. The impression that it was an actual structure, is also supported by an article on the venue that appeared in *Shoreham Glories (In Scraps and Stories)* by an author simply named "William", wherein it states:

> Come on! You sons-of-energy; lets climb the Castle of Falkenstein and get the view.

The answer, of course, was staring us in the face, for several prints of the area, included in Sickelmore's Guide Book, show a slender turret or tower that is clearly identified as the Observatory. This building, with a viewing platform at the top, has a markedly Gothic appearance, which, bearing in mind the previous quotation from *Shoreham Glories (In Scraps and Stories)* convinces us it was also known as the Castle of Falkenstein? Indeed, that may always have been its name, the term, Observatory, might only have related to the viewing platform?

This is purely conjecture, but should we be right, Mr Ruff's connection is easily explained. He was a local artist, so it seems safe to assume that the tower would be portrayed in some of his works, and if it was known to him as the Castle of Falkenstein, that presumably is what it would have been called in the Diorama Exhibition. But why the place was called 'Falkenstein' is another mystery. We can only suggest that it was a play on the name 'Frankenstein' and taken from *Frankenstein, or the modern Prometheus,* the title of Mary Shelley's popular novel that had been published a few years earlier.

Whilst on the subject of architecture, a little more should be said about the main buildings in the gardens. For instance, who could have failed to be impressed by the magnificent, twin-towered entrance pavilion, or the Swiss Cottage itself – so well described in Sickelmore's Guide. This was built entirely of Stockholm timber, and for many years was regarded as the finest example of such workmanship to be found anywhere in the country. The ballroom too, which was built in 1878, was another example of Victorian excellence. According to *The Book of Brighton, As it was and as it is. And Talkee – Talkee,* it measured 200 feet long and 70 feet wide, although other accounts differ, saying 150 feet long and 54 feet wide. But it matters not, for while different writers may disagree with regard to the dimensions, they are as one in their approval, claiming that it was the best such venue to be found anywhere on the south coast.

Entrance to the Swiss Gardens (approx 1928) – The original venue had closed long before this photograph was taken, however the entrance remained on site for many years, and the lake, although greatly reduced in size, was still available for boat hire.

A poster advertising a performance at the Swiss Gardens theatre

In *The Story of Shoreham,* author, Henry Cheal, when referring to the ballroom, stated:

> Here a former generation of Shoreham and Brighton people were wont to trip it right merrily, celebrating the successful launch of a new-built ship, or as a suitable wind-up to Regatta Day.

Later, when speaking more generally about the Gardens, he went on:

> In those days they were also considered a part of the social life of the town, and it was the usual fashion to meet friends and take tea with them, in one of the delightful arbours which were to be found there. The evening performance in the theatre followed, and then the dance in the ballroom.

A tea ticket

Opposite page: The new ballroom (the most famous of the Gardens pavilions) and the New Lodge. Rebuilt to the designs of Arthur Loader between 1876 and 1878

NEW BALL ROOM & LODGE ✳ SWISS GARDENS ✳ NEW SHOREHAM ✳ SUS.

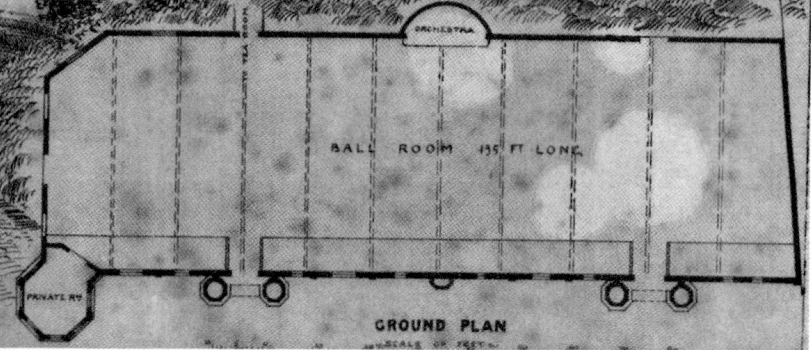

BALL ROOM 135 FT LONG.

ORCHESTRA

PRIVATE RY

GROUND PLAN

This atmospheric photograph pinpoints the position of the Gardens in relation to the town and its surroundings. The chapel to Lancing College can just be seen silhouetted in the background, and those with a keen eye may be able to pick out the old wooden bridge crossing the river.

A view of the lake in later days

The Swiss Gardens then, by any measure, were the most successful and influential of all the Sussex Pleasure Grounds. They remained open for 67 years, the first 50 of which were a continuous hey-day, after which, standards slowly began to slip. Following Mr Balley, the proprietorship vested in Mr Edward Goodchild, and after him, passed through a number of hands, including, but not necessarily in this order: J. B. and G. Mallison, Mr G. Reeves Smith, Henry Boleno, Hubbard and King, and Ind Coope and Co.

After which, according to Henry Cheal:

> ...came the days when the Gardens were entirely closed to the public, nature alone held sway there and had her own way with them, and a beautiful way it was too. Surely, never in former times, when so carefully tended by expert gardeners, had they appeared so lovely.

This photograph of the grounds (taken after the closure) shows the ruined remains of a glasshouse, which one imagines was heated, as there appears to be an iron chimney-stack projecting through the roof.

Mr Loader's new Ballroom – prior to demolition

41

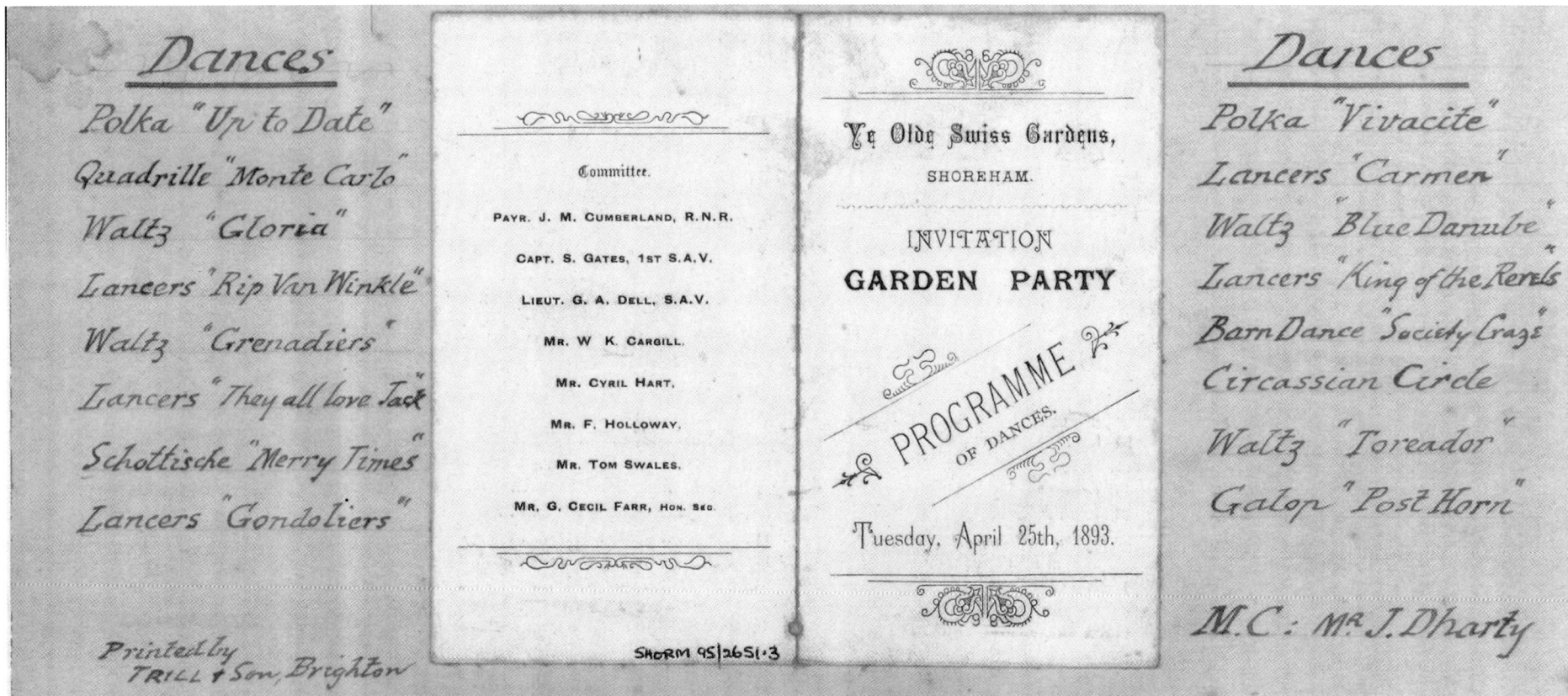

Dances

Polka "Up to Date"

Quadrille "Monte Carlo"

Waltz "Gloria"

Lancers "Rip Van Winkle"

Waltz "Grenadiers"

Lancers "They all love Jack"

Schottische "Merry Times"

Lancers "Gondoliers"

Printed by
TRILL & Son, Brighton

Committee.

PAYR. J. M. CUMBERLAND, R.N.R.

CAPT. S. GATES, 1ST S.A.V.

LIEUT. G. A. DELL, S.A.V.

MR. W. K. CARGILL.

MR. CYRIL HART.

MR. F. HOLLOWAY.

MR. TOM SWALES.

MR. G. CECIL FARR, HON. SEC.

SHORM 95/2651·3

Ye Olde Swiss Gardens,

SHOREHAM.

INVITATION

GARDEN PARTY

PROGRAMME
OF DANCES.

Tuesday, April 25th, 1893.

Dances

Polka "Vivacité"

Lancers "Carmen"

Waltz "Blue Danube"

Lancers "King of the Revels"

Barn Dance "Society Craze"

Circassian Circle

Waltz "Toreador"

Galop "Post Horn"

M.C: Mr J. Dharty

An invitation to a Garden Party at 'Ye Olde Swiss Gardens'.

Then with the predictability of night following day, demolition men levelled the place to the ground, and to the distress of many, a landmark they had known and loved for all their lives, disappeared for ever. We, thank goodness, can avoid such a gloomy ending, and via the medium of the printed word, return again to the golden days of the Gardens, and there take our leave by quoting, this time in full, the cheerful extract from *Shoreham Glories (In Scraps and Stories)* by 'William':

Ye Olde Swisse Gardens (Days of Glory: 1875-1890)

"Come on! Brightonians; roll over to Shoreham!

Bank Holiday! Glorious weather, and a Grand Fete on!

Horse-brakes, two shillings a seat; open landaus, twelve shillings for four, or one shilling by train, including admission!

For a penny more, railway-travellers can take the horse-tram from Shoreham station, yes, right along the Western Road!

What if she comes off the rails at Gigins Corner?

You'll be "off the rails" too, before you get back!

besides, it'll give you a chance at the 'Burrell', or the "Buck". Then, at journey's-end, you can pop into the 'Hebe'…"

(Later: after 'Hebe' refreshments)

"Come on! Let's go into the Gardens now; jolly spot, isn't it?

And what a smashing band.

We'll have a row on the lake later; how cool it looks!

Who cares if the boat goes over? We can chase the ducks then! Mine's the brown one with the white tail!

Come on! You sons-of-energy; let's climb the castle of Falkenstein and get the view; we can see the balloon go up from there too!

(Later: from the top)

Phew! What a height! What a picture! This is Switzerland!

(We'll get an avalanche too; if this lot gives way!)

Doesn't the ballroom over there look swell, and the temple!

Who's it erected to, I wonder: Bacchus or Cupid? – Cupid I reckon; there's a lot of couples about!

Hullo! The band's marching over for tonight's dance.

There won't half be a crowd! I'll bet Frankie the Butcher*

is there! I'll bet we all enjoy ourselves too!

What matter if we sway a bit, when we be done?

That'll be the dancing has made us giddy!

besides we can all get a sixpenny flower bunch to take home, for a peace offering.

Yes, get it at Strawberry Lodge; that little shop we pass in Southdown Road.

If we miss the last train back we'll take the horse-tram to Hove, and walk the rest.

The fresh air will do us good.

*Frankie the Butcher – a famous Shoreham character.

The Swiss Gardens Theatre – "The Last Act"

The Chinese Gardens

The success of the Shoreham resort caused many an aspiring entrepreneur to reconsider investing in public pleasure gardens. One such man was Adam Adams. Every spring and summer Bank Holiday he saw great numbers of Brighton folk, who, weary of their bleak, windswept and virtually treeless town, had travelled up the road from the coast, intent on a day of picnicking and fun, in the beautiful Wealden countryside. Equally, he was aware that it was only a matter of time before the London to Brighton Railway Line (already in an advanced stage of construction) would be operating, thus making the area more accessible. Opportunity beckoned, and Mr Adams responded.

He decided that he would open a venue after the style of the Swiss Gardens and that Hurstpierpoint would be the ideal location. The district was a good choice for many reasons, not the least being that although predominantly rural , it was also a prosperous, bustling community with six public-houses, a brewery, two blacksmiths and a local fire brigade. Added to this, it was well connected by road, as London to Brighton coaches passed through the village several times daily. The railway station at Hassocks would be within reasonable walking distance, and those unable to do so, or who were not prepared to make the effort, could be conveyed hither and thither by wagonette.

The resort was called the Chinese Gardens, not for any romantic or fashionable reason, but simply because of its establishment in Chinese Road (later changed to Western Road) a title which was derived from the Chinese uprising. This sort of parlance was quite common in the Victorian era, when many houses, roads etc were named after the numerous military conflicts and engagements in which our country had participated. Therefore we are able to declare, that, despite the connotations suggested by the name, there was nothing particularly oriental about the Gardens. Mr Adams opened for business on the 19th June, 1843, just five years after the Swiss Gardens, but it would appear that the elements rather spoilt his big day, for a covering article in the *Sussex Agricultural Express* stated:

Chinese Gardens
Hotel and
Pleasure Grounds

Hurstpierpoint

Sussex

Fully Licensed

TELEPHONE 2241

A brochure cover for the Chinese Gardens

The Chinese Gardens, Hurstpierpoint – an early photograph

Opening of the Chinese Gardens, Hurstpierpoint

The above gardens were opened on Monday the 19th inst., but in consequence of the weather being unfavourable, the attendance of visitors was not so numerous as was anticipated; not withstanding a most respectable company was present to witness the proceedings of the occasion, which elicited the approbation of the spectators. The gardens which appear to be in a very forward state and the recreations it will afford, prove that there is every probability of its becoming a favourite summer resort. We are glad to find the proprietor has begun with spirit, and hope ere long success will crown his efforts.

These hopes were soon realised, for visitors from all over the county flocked to the site, where they found they could row on a lake, enjoy donkey rides, participate in games of bowls, croquet and tennis, or perhaps just stroll about the grounds.

During the following year, 1884, Mr Adams placed an advertisement in the *Sussex Agricultural Express*, which read:

Chinese Gardens, Hurstpierpoint

A. Adams begs respectfully to inform the public that the OPENING OF THE ABOVE PLEASURE GARDENS will take place on Whit Monday, the 27th of May, 1844, and continue open every day throughout the summer. Schools and tea parties will find every accomodation and attention, their comforts in every respect having been completely studied.

In a supporting article, the same newspaper commented:

We understand that these gardens, which are very tastefully laid out, are well worth a visit from the soujourners at Brighton and other places in the neighbourhood, for, independently of their immediate attractions, the rural scenery of this place cannot fail to call forth the admiration of all lovers of nature.

The Gardens then, though never seriously rivalling their southern neighbour, swiftly established themselves as a popular venue, and it became a virtual tradition that groups of holiday-makers, intent on visiting Brighton and other seaside towns, would break their journey at Hurstpierpoint for lunch and beverages, or perhaps stop for tea on the homeward run.

The Chinese Gardens in the 1930s – having undergone considerable renovation

This photograph, taken in the early 1920s, shows the lawn at the rear of the hotel, and the landlord's wife, Mrs Pearn, feeding ducks. The single-storey building in the centre was used as a weekend cinema during and after the Second World War.

The lake at the Chinese Gardens

The lawns and playing fields at the Chinese Gardens, an area that is now completely covered in housing.

On Wednesday, the members of the Sunday School, the Band of Hope, the Temperance Society and the Drum and Fife Band, in connection with the Thomas Street Mission, Brighton, had an excursion to the Chinese Gardens, Hurstpierpoint. The party numbered about 500, and left Kemp Town by special train at 9.55am. From Hassocks Station the visitors went to the Gardens in wagons, wagonettes etc., with the exception of a few who preferred to walk, and the band played nearly all the way. At the Gardens the usual games were indulged in by young and old, and races were also arranged. Tea was provided for the party, and the Rev. H. Shearer addressed a few words. After tea, various groups were photographed and prizes were distributed by the Rev. gentleman.

The size of the grounds (which was considerable) can be readily gauged when one learns that in addition to a wooded area, there were five and a half acres of parkland, a three-acre field containing a cricket pitch, a huge lawn for general sporting activities, a three-quarter acre boating lake and a lily pond.

Bands played throughout the day, while side amusements included the aforementioned donkey rides, boat-swings, plank swings, a shooting gallery, archery and darts.

The general accomodation comprised of public bars, a saloon bar and a coffee room. A main dining hall could seat up to three hundred guests, and an enclosure could cater for two hundred more. This arrangement made it possible to segregate wine drinking and temperance parties, whose visits sometimes clashed! Ladies and gentlemen's lavatories, suitably staffed by attendants, were also provided.

A typical example of an excursion to the Grounds was contained in the *Mid Sussex Times*, dated 30-6-1891, wherein it was reported:

1913 – Children from the Ansty 'Band of Hope' en route to their Annual Treat at the Chinese Gardens

1919 – This could fairly be described as a busman's holiday, for the group pictured here in the grounds of the Chinese Gardens, were members of the stage staff from Devonshire Park Theatre, at Eastbourne.

Over the years, various proprietors continued to maintain the high standard set by Mr Adams, and amongst these are some well remembered names, such as Mr and Mrs H. L. V. Pearn and Mrs C. Goode. Unfortunately, towards the end of the last named lady's turn at the helm, an indication that all was not well appeared in the final sentence of a Gardens brochure. We have reproduced the document in full, because, apart from anything else, it provides a good feel of the times:

> The Chinese Gardens are unique for outings and beanfeast parties, and being off the main road there is no interference from passing traffic, and parties of a large size are able to book the whole place exclusively by arrangement.
>
> The accommodation is ideal for firms and clubs, who prefer to spend their whole day together with games and sports, instead of going to the adjacent coastal towns, where they generally get much distributed. Dancing and singing is permitted after tea. Pianos provided and amplified 'Gram'.
>
> The huge Parking Ground will accommodate sixty charabancs with at least two hundred private cars. The whole premises are lighted by electricity. A photographer is always in attendance for taking groups etc. Pictures are printed and ready for you to take away at 5 o'clock each day. Presents and Brighton Rock can be purchased just before you leave.

> A hearty welcome awaits all visiting parties, and the proprietors pay very personal attention to service and quality, and every effort is made to make the day a happy one for all. We, in our turn like parties visiting here to assist us to conduct our business as required by law.

Sadly, there were excellent reasons for the underlining, for during the 1930s, the Gardens became a focal point for groups of people whose idea of a good day out, was to spend it in a state of inebriation. In consequence, the hoarse bellowing of drunks was frequently heard, while fighting and threatening behaviour became a regular and wholly unwelcome feature of the neighbourhood. Not surprisingly, respectable visitors deserted the venue in droves, and despite efforts by the management to deal with the situation, things were never the same again, the gloss had gone, and this was increasingly reflected in the general appearance of the establishment. Grass verges remained untrimmed, there were oily puddles in the car park, and the whole place showed increasing signs of neglect.

Under the cover of darkness, local hooligans entered the grounds and threw furniture into the lake, or committed other mindless acts of vandalism, while drunks remained a persistent nuisance. They targeted their abuse on one attraction in particular. This stood at the entrance of the Gardens and consisted of a Chimpanzees Tea Party carved in stone. Beautifully executed, and immensely heavy, the creatures were the work of a Mr Stanley Anscombe, a local craftsman, of whom it had been said: "He could turn his hand to anything."

One Saturday night, according to an old village resident, a group of intoxicated East-Enders spilled out of the pub and thought it would be a 'good wheeze' to load the chimps into their coach. The remarks uttered upon discovering the sheer weight of the animals is better left to the imagination, but undeterred, they somehow managed to drag about three of the statues on board. After which, with clothing scuffed and fingernails broken, they stood back gasping for breath and gleefully congratulated each other on their cleverness.

However, the glory of the moment was short lived, for unknown to them, their exertions had been observed by the village constable, Arthur Durrant. He was no paper-pushing policeman, but one of the old school, who would as soon wrap his cape round a ruffian's ear than pull out his pocket book. Waiting then until the task was completed, he stepped out of the shadows, and announced in a voice that broked no dissent:

"Right! – either them monkeys" (pointing to the stone figures silhouetted within the coach) "gets put back – or you monkeys!" (pointing to the startled Londoners) "gets nicked!"

Despite competition from cinema and radio, and even the advent of television, the Chinese Gardens soldiered on, albeit in a reduced capacity, until the 1950s. Then, approximately 110 years after their opening, the famous old grounds (which by now were greatly reduced in size) closed for the last time.

The public-house continued to function in a somewhat desultory fashion and in an effort to re-establish its fortunes the brewers gave the place a 'fresh lick of paint' and changed the name to the 'Pierpoint'. But it was too little and too late, and like the gardens, all trace of its existence has long since vanished.

The Duke of Norfolk and Officers of the 4th Battalion, Royal Sussex Regiment at a recruitment parade held at the Chinese Gardens (circa 1910)

The Victoria Gardens, 1924 to 1939

This venue was the subject of an earlier book[1] which dealt with the life and times of the first proprietor (our maternal grandfather) Edwin Street. The narrative ending with his death in 1923. However, the Gardens, which were inherited by his daughter, Mrs Daisy Florence Upton, continued to function until the outbreak of the Second World War. What follows is a brief account of those days.

Standing six foot four inches in his stockinged feet and weighing just under 25 stones, Edwin Street was a conspicuous figure. As well as being the proprietor of what in their heyday were considered to have been the finest pleasure gardens on the south coast, he was also one of the best known farmers in the county, the premier butcher in the district, and a long serving and outspoken independent member of Burgess Hill Town Council. Reports of his sudden and unexpected death were initially greeted with disbelief, and such was the strength of his personality, that he remained a subject of comment in local newspapers for a long time to come. A brief but warm-hearted reference in the *Mid Sussex Times* a few years later illustrates this nicely:

> A great number of people from Brighton, Mid-Sussex, and elsewhere entered the Victoria Pleasure Gardens on Easter Monday. Many still missed the genial presence of the late Mr Edwin Street, who had been the proprietor ever since the Gardens were started as such, but Mrs Upton, and other members of the Street family were there with an adequate staff, and all the visitors were well catered for.

Their unrivalled reputation, together with the sheer size of the grounds, and the fact that they had provided pleasure for the masses for more years than most people could remember, still made the Victoria Gardens an automatic

Daisy Florence Upton, who inherited the proprietorship of the Victoria Pleasure Gardens from her father, Edwin Street

[1] Edwin Street and the Victoria Pleasure Gardens

52

Although taken a little earlier than the times depicted, this photograph of a Sunday School group, marching up Trafalgar Street to Brighton Railway Station en route to Burgess Hill, gives a good idea of the size of the crowds that visited the Gardens.

choice for any large public gathering. So it was not surprising that it was chosen for the 1924 Burgess Hill Allied Sports Fete. This was a big event and a real test for the new proprietor in her first full season. Vast crowds were expected to attend, and according to the *Mid Sussex Times*, a varied programme would include:

> ...races for all, tug of war, tilting the bucket, a Punch and Judy Show, coconut shies, hoop-la, judging a pigs weight, a bowling competition, magic mirrors, boating on the lake, roundabouts, swing-boats, music by Burgess Hill Town Band, and during the evening, dancing in the pavilion.
>
> Thousands of people are expected from all parts of Sussex, and cheap tickets will be issued by Southern Railway.

The great day arrived, the weather was perfect, and as predicted, thousands of people did come, causing the turn-stiles to rattle continuously from 9 am onwards. There was only one casualty, during the day when a boat capsized in the lake, and its occupant was covered in slime and weeds!

Youngsters from various organisations queuing up in the driveway that led from London Road to the Gardens

Back in the early 1920s, Edwin Street had clearly foreseen a trend. A great believer in giving people what they wanted, and convinced that 'moving pictures' were the coming thing, he intended to hold regular film shows at the grounds, and then in due course, to construct a modern cinema on the site. Such up-to-date facilities, he reasoned, would regain for the venue its former proud position as the main entertainment centre in the south. He was actually engaged in setting it up – seating had been purchased, also a projector, a big screen, even a number of Charlie Chaplin films – when death, with scant regard for the best laid plans, took him unexpectedly, and the grand vision of a second cinema in Burgess Hill perished with our grandfather.

But with his daughter, Daisy, at the helm, business remained brisk, and visitors still came on a regular basis. The fact that the place remained a temperance resort helped, for in those days societies opposed to 'demon drink' were well supported, as were church groups, and so during the summer weekends, crowds of fun-seekers, young and old, still made their way from the railway station to the Gardens.

The following account written by Eileen Hallett (daughter of Daisy Upton) is a remembrance of those times. It originally appeared in journal number three of the Burgess Hill Local History Society

> My first memories of the Gardens stretch back to the late 1920s. The season started in early summer and lasted through until the end of August. The largest parties, which were mostly Sunday Schools, came on Wednesdays and Saturdays, these would number as many as six to eight hundred children a time, so there was a mammoth task of catering to be done. By 8 o'clock in the morning, the large coppers were lit, these were fuelled with logs and faggots, the wood pile and faggot stack being at the back of the Tea Rooms. The kitchen was very primitive compared with today's standards. It consisted of a large room fitted between and connected with, two former railway carriages, these were used as store-rooms. There was also a small room called the 'ice-safe', this had a brick floor and was kept cool by large blocks of ice weighing about half a hundredweight each. In the actual kitchen there were two shallow sinks, two gas stoves, a large dresser and a big wooden table where the staff had their lunch, and of course we always joined them. The meal was usually cold silverside of beef, potatoes and pickles, followed by treacle pudding or spotted dog

1925 – A visit to the Victoria Gardens by the 'Sons of Temperance'

covered with butter and sugar. There were other things as well, but these stick in my memory, because they were my favourites.

Filled to capacity, the main dining room could accommodate over a thousand people and was fitted with trestle tables and forms. Tea for the children consisted of slices of bread and butter. This was all cut by hand during the morning and packed away in big boxes. Then in the afternoon it was served with strawberry or apricot jam and slices of Dundee and Madeira cake, which was supplied by the Crawley Cake Company. The tea was made in urns, then taken round the tables in enamel jugs, and this was quite a task when there were several hundred cups to fill. The adults had their refreshments separately from the children, with pots of tea, cucumber and tomatoes.

Hot water from the coppers was ladled into large galvanised baths for washing the dishes and cutlery. The drying up was done with immensely long table cloths, everyone using a couple of yards or so.

Many of the outings came by train and a really brave sight were the Co-op Guilds. They came from all parts of Sussex and marched down from the station with their banners flying, then assembled in the evening to march back again. We would sit on the turnstile to watch them go. I say 'we' as beside my brothers and myself, there were usually two or three school friends or cousins with us most days. My mother was so used to dealing with large numbers that she didn't really mind if her own family seemed to double or treble, and there was always plenty of bread and butter in the boxes.

Most of the visiting groups had sports in the afternoons. There were egg and spoon races, sack races, bat and trap, cricket and stoolball. Sometimes pennies would be thrown up in the air and children would scramble for them. Occasionally there would be parties of campers. One such group, the Maid's Brigade I believe, were accompanied by a curate, and while his back was turned, the girls shut one of our donkeys in his tent. The poor man was not at all amused, and departed in a terrible huff.

People always wanted to go on the lake and there was a variety of craft to choose from, flat-bottomed paddle canoes, skiffs and large

Staff in the dining room at the time of the Exhibition of Art and Industry. The lady to the right of the photograph was Mary Faccenda, daughter of Mr Faccenda, who ran the ice cream kiosk at the premises.

rowing boats that could hold up to thirty children. My mother, who was experienced in such matters, always had a good supply of spare clothing for those who fell in! This happened more frequently than not, but there was no real danger, the water was shallow and it was just a case of a good towelling down, a change of clothes and no one any the worse.

Sometimes a Sunday School party would sing hymns when they were out on the lake, and it really sounded rather pleasant. I remember once – probably because it was so appropriate – they sang, "We are but the Fishers of Men", and thought to myself what fun it would be, if one of them had fallen overboard!

On one occasion, visitors to the Gardens discovered a new attraction awaiting them. It was Whippet racing: Burgess Hill's new sport according to the *Mid Sussex Times*.

Whippet racing is very popular in various parts of the country [the paper claimed] and it was introduced to Burgess Hill for the first

1930 – The boating lake at the Victoria Gardens. The oarswoman was a local lady by the name of Kathy Kettle.

time on Saturday. Mr R. de Caux and Mr S. Upton (Daisy's husband) were responsible for the organisation and they had the satisfaction of seeing a large entry and some good racing. If another meeting is held on August Bank Holiday, as has been suggested, there is no doubt of it being very successful.

Such a meeting was held and it was very successful, over 1,200 sporting ladies and gentlemen attended. The atmosphere was all that could be expected. Tipsters abounded. Bookies shouted the odds, and an enthusiastic and noisy crowd cheered on the favourites. However, it was never to be repeated, why we are not sure, but possibly because the authorities feared that undesirable characters would be attracted to the area.

"The event of the season" (trumpeted the *Mid Sussex Times*) will be a Great Exhibition of Art and Industries to be held at the Victoria Gardens, Burgess Hill, between Wednesday, May 9th and Saturday, May 12th, 1926 – you really must pay a visit!

The object of the Exhibition was twofold. First, to discover any hitherto unknown talent in the district. Second, to provide financial aid for local institutions.

To the gratification of the promoters, the public responded to the invitation with great enthusiasm. The event was mainly staged in the large pavilion, and the building could have been constructed for the purpose, so great was the number and variety of the exhibits. Diverse and fascinating items from far and wide were examined by countless pairs of curious eyes. Here one could read a London Gazette dated 1695, or study the first Bradshaw Railway Guide ever published. One could sit on a tiger-skin from Bengal, gaze at a stuffed mongoose attacking a stuffed cobra, hold the golden key to Brighton's Clock Tower, or reverently inspect the ragged remains of HMS Victory's flag (shot to shreds when Nelson died). There was a pair of

The Burgess Hill and District Electric Supply Company Ltd at the Exhibition of Art and Industry

The Burgess Hill and St John's Common Gas Company at the Exhibition of Art and Industry

These little animals were real characters, with names like 'Searchlight', 'Jack' and 'Brownie'. Sometimes they would be joined by a pony called 'Spider' who was hired out by Mr Twose, a local farmer. Jack in particular was a real free spirit, and on one occasion refused to be caught. He led his pursuers all the way up to London Road, where he rolled on his back in the middle of the highway. Then, having demonstrated his independence, he jumped up, brayed triumphantly, and trotted, docilely back to the Gardens.

No welcoming smiles from this grim-faced group standing by the entrance gate to the Gardens

scales for weighing guineas, a model of the Taj Mahal, needlework by John Constable's aunt, a Tibetan prayer wheel, and a curious old clock from Lewes Prison. In addition there were examples of printing by Hilary Peplar, and carpentry by George Maxwell (both of whom were members of the Guild of St. Joseph and St. Dominic on Ditchling Common). Specimens of weaving were exhibited by John Killick, while some fine etching, silver-smithing, lithographic and lacquor work were loaned for display by the Brighton Municipal School of Art.

The Trade Section added considerably to the general effect of the Exhibition. Great interest was displayed in the Burgess Hill and St John's Gas Company's stall, there people could see a gas meter at work – and inspect the the latest thing in ovens. Not to be outdone, the Electricity Company had a brilliantly illuminated stand with flashing lights, while a craftsman from W. Meeds and Son, drew gasps of amazement from the public, who constantly surrounding him, marvelled at the deft way in which he operated the potter's wheel. Mr Atkins, a Burgess Hill optician, displayed scientific instruments together with an exquisite range of tortoiseshell framed spectacles. And virtually everything from tables to teaspoons was exhibited by Hoadley's, the town's major departmental store. That was not all, the latest type of portable wireless sets and other equipment was put on show by a firm called Burgess Hill Radio Supplies, and Mr A. J. Mighell, a local building and decorating contractor, erected a full size model of a room, containing a door fitted with what was described as an ingenious device for the delivery of parcels and milk!

As their contribution to the proceedings, the London Road Infants School produced a May Revels each afternoon. This consisted of the children giving little recitals, singing and dancing, and concluding with a traditional dance round the maypole. Concerts were held in the evenings, and on the last night there was a musical extravanganza attended by special guests. The final feature (warmly recalled by one who was there) was a particularly jolly dance entitled, "We won't go home till morning".

Referring back to the earlier account of the Allied Sports Fete, readers may recall that mention was made of an unfortunate man, who after tumbling into the lake, was pulled out covered in slime and weeds. The fact that it was possible for such an accident to occur, was probably the only drawback of the venue. The problem was caused by the poplar trees that lined the water's edge. During the autumn, they shed nearly all of their leaves onto its surface, these sank to the bottom and decomposed into a putrid mess. If left to nature, the lake would have eventually silted up and turned into an evil smelling bog. To avoid such a thing happening, regular action was required, and precisely what was done is described by Eileen Hallett:

> Every so often the lake had to be dredged, this was quite a performance. The men would row from one side to the other, and drop a huge wooden rake into the water, this was attached to a long chain, and they would then return to the far bank, jump ashore, heave on the chain, and gradually drag the contrivance, together with an ever increasing quantity of black mud and weed, back across the bottom of the lake to where they stood. We children used to help (or perhaps hinder!). for I can remember one of my cousins getting a smart clip round the ear, when his absolutely filthy hands slipped off the chain, and onto the arm of the man standing next to him.

> The sediment was deposited between the poplar trees, and in time, turned into a rich, loamy soil full of tiny shells.

Sundays during the season were generally considered to be the favourite day for visits by group outings, not least because of the splendid meals that were prepared by Mrs Upton for her guests. But being that it was a teetotal establishment, there were always those who arrived late because of delays encountered at various hostelries along the way, with the result that when the charabancs did eventually roll in, the occupants who disembarked, although full of high spirits were in no condition to enjoy the fare provided.

One hot August weekend, the members of a working-men's club, after a valiant attempt to drink "Burgess Hill dry", staggered into the grounds, clutching crates of IPA, and with boozy good cheer, decided that the first thing to do, was to go on the lake. Then, when the exercise of rowing sent their temperatures soaring, they concluded that the second thing to do, was go into the lake! So raucously cheering, they rose unsteadily to their feet, and whilst shocked onlookers averted their eyes, the voyagers pulled off their clothes and flopped naked into the water.

It was only by great good fortune that their visit did not coincide with the annual works outing held by the ladies from Hambrooks Pickle Factory. Having arrived at Burgess Hill, these East End Amazons (led apparently by a gigantic woman dressed like a costermonger) first consumed vast

Mr Antonio Faccenda's Ice Cream Kiosk. Of Italian extraction, Mr Faccenda had been associated with the Victoria Gardens since their opening in 1897. His children obviously inherited his business acumen, as one son, Joseph, had fishmonger's shops in Ditchling and Hurstpierpoint. Another son, Salvatore ('Saddle') ran an ice delivery service from Brighton, whilst yet another son, Emilio, was the proprietor of the Farmer's Stores in West Street, Burgess Hill.

amounts of beer both at the Potters and the Brewers Arms (where for some reason they removed all the light bulbs) and then, having drunk their fill, descended upon the Gardens and created absolute pandemonium.

These quite definitely were not the sort of customers Mrs Upton wished to welcome, and following numerous complaints from local residents, she decided that her only course of action was to close the premises on Sundays.

Several independent little businesses flourished within the confines of the Gardens. For instance, there was an ice cream kiosk fitted with containers that had shiny brass lids. This was owned and operated by a Mr Faccenda (a stalwart of many years standing at the resort) and the ice cream he served his customers was made to his own special recipe. Such was its quality and reputation, that he also supplied the Chinese Gardens at Hurstpierpoint, and the Orchard Gardens at Hassocks, and his 'Stop Me and Buy One' tricycle with its tinkling bell, was a familiar sight and sound on Mid Sussex roads.

Then there was the famous cycle track. This had been run by Mr William Wheatley (photographer, bill poster, and man of many parts) since the grounds first opened in 1897, and the hiring of bicycles and three wheelers was as popular as ever. They came in all sizes and were painted every colour under the sun, most of the machines being clearly marked with their

The roundabout at the Victoria Gardens

own individual names. Every child in Burgess Hill knew that if you could generate sufficient speed on old Wheatley's trikes, it was possible to take the corner of the track on two wheels, which was a tremendous thrill and the hallmark of a real dare-devil. Even some of the mothers were tempted to have a go, especially if they had just enjoyed a liquid lunch at the Brewers Arms!

In 1935, the Orchard Gardens at Hassocks closed, and a family named Shippobottam, who lived in a caravan at the grounds, and ran various sideshows there (including a cycle roundabout) transferred their business to Burgess Hill. Margate was both their home town and winter quarters, but on Easter Bank Holiday weekend, they would arrive at Mrs Upton's resort, take up residence in a shed, and for the rest of the season, look after the coconut shies, the tumbling tanks, and a 'test your strength' machine. They were pleasant people, although a little mysterious, none more so than Mr Shippobottam, a dapper, rather insignificant little man, who only showed up occasionally, and whose business card proclaimed him to be:

> Professor Ohmy – specialist in:
>
> Curing stammering, smoky chimneys, teaching ornamental swimming, saw sharpening, carpentry, joiners work, exhibition and shop fitting. Now solving the superadio problem of vibrations and oscillations.

The Shippobottams outside the little hut that served as their living quarters throughout the season

The resident photographer, Mr Stan Groves, was another who made his living at the Grounds. He must have recorded thousands of happy moments for posterity, and is chiefly remembered for the amusing and imaginative props that he used. Two screens in particular come to mind, one being a life size reproduction of the famous Pears Soap advertisement, 'Bubbles', and the other showed two pugilists trading blows. In each case, the heads of the characters depicted had been carefully cut out, which made it possible for the customers standing behind, to poke their own heads through instead!

While events in the outside world were gathering apace, life at the Gardens carried on much as it had done since our grandfather's death. Dances and concerts remained a regular feature throughout the year. Large companies and organisations, such as Allan West, Brighton Post Office and the Brighton Workhouse still had their outings there. Fetes and sporting events continued to be staged at the grounds, and with regards to the latter, it is worth recording that St. Dunstan's Home for the Blind actually held a sports day in the big hall (ropes being stretched from one end of the room to the other to guide those taking part). Burgess Hill Football Club played its home matches at the Victoria Gardens. Boy scouts camped in the fields during the summer and if conditions permitted there was ice skating on the lake in the winter. There was even the occasional duck shoot but according to someone who took part, these would appear to have been rather ill-planned affairs:

> "I always remember," he said, "when Syd Upton decided to have a duck shoot one Saturday, and we built some blinds to fire from – the first shots scared the birds so much that they flew down to New Close. Old Tom Scrase was sent after them in his car and told to let off a couple of barrels, then to high tail it back to the Gardens before the ducks got there – I don't think it was a very successful operation!"

Ice skating on the lake

Suddenly it was 1939, once again England was at war with Germany, and for the second time in their history, the Gardens were taken over by the military authorities. It must have been with a real sense of *déjà vu* that Mrs Upton closed the gates for the last time, for the place had been her life. As a little girl she could remember her parents' high hopes when the venue first opened and the excitement of the great days that followed. As a young woman she clearly recalled the shock of the enforced enclosure in 1914, the destruction caused by the occupying troops and the hard work that was required to make the eventual re-opening the success it was – a success so nearly turned to ashes by her father's unexpected death. But undeterred, she had taken on the responsibility of running the resort herself, and raised three children in the process. The demands, however, were great, and the second closure when it came, proved to be the final straw, the heart went out of her – and the Gardens never re-opened again.

Youngsters having descended the slide, Eileen Hallett is on the far left of the picture. She still retains a vivid memory of a fat lady becoming stuck half way down – "The more she struggled to get free, the more tightly she became wedged in. It was difficult to get to her, and it seemed like ages before she was rescued."

A troupe of Spanish girls, refugees from their country because of the Civil War, who visited the Gardens in 1938 and entertained the local people with the music and song of their homeland.

The 1970s – Draining the lake in preparation for the extension of the factory estate. In the background, partly concealed by trees, is a last glimpse of Edwin Street's great hall.

During the reconstruction programme, the stream that originally fed the lake was piped underground.
This photograph was taken from where it now flows beneath Albert Drive.

Some of the poplar trees that lined the southern shore of the lake (planted by Edwin Street in 1900) can still be seen today, albeit in very different surroundings.

These were the former Hedgecock girl – five sisters from Brighton, who together with their brothers, regularly visited the Victoria Gardens on Sunday school outings during the 1930s. One of them, Mrs Peggy Brooker, when recalling her childhood, commented:

"We thought that there was nothing else on earth like it. In the first field there were swings, they were funny because they didn't have chains to hold, just two straight rods of iron. In the next field was a lovely big wooden slide with lino nailed to it, and we came sliding down on bits of matting. Near the lake was a large hut which contained penny amusements, and outside you could hire boats. A path through the hedge led to the cycle track where there were all sorts of bikes, and for a penny you could go round three or four times (not owning bikes ourselves made this a special treat). Then it was over the little rustic bridge to the other side of the lake for sport and races. Those trips to Burgess Hill were magic days out for us."

The Orchard Pleasure Gardens

Skirting clumps of blackthorn, the path from Kings Drive wound its way through a wasteland of thistles, and ended abruptly at the top of some cement steps which descended to a huge rectangular depression in the ground. This was man-made and must have measured at least 150 yards long by 30 yards wide – possibly more. The sides and base were concreted and the entire area reeked of abandonment and decay. Brambles trailed down the walls, ferns sprouted in crevices and cracks, while docks and other forms of rank growth forced its way up through the floor.

Positioned rather incongruously in the centre of this dried-out lake (for that assuredly is what it was) stood a small island, so overgrown as to be impenetrable. Some fancy shrubs and a rustic shed for wildfowl, that once must have presented such an attractive picture, were completely smothered by willow, elderberry and great clusters of stinging nettles, the roots of which coiled out of the crumbling banks like obscene yellow serpents.

I did not realise at the time, but this gloomy spot was all that remained of the old Orchard Pleasure Gardens, a place that in its day had been one of the most popular holiday resorts in the county.

(Extract from The Old Century *by Mark Dudeney)*

The affection that Brighton's townsfolk felt for the neighbourhood of Mid Sussex was unabating. We already know that specially commissioned trains were required to transport the vast crowds that wished to come up for a day, and not just with the purpose of visiting the Pleasure Gardens, many remained loyal to the old tradition of simply enjoying the freedom of the fields and woods, of exploring and picnicking, and gathering bunches of flowers to take home. A rather alarming picture regarding this last mentioned activity can be found in *Edwin Street and the Victoria Pleasure Gardens*. wherein it states:

> …like a swarm of locusts, they [the visitors] virtually stripped the woods and meadows of every sprig and blossom to be seen. And as if that wasn't enough, after they had gone, bluebells, primroses and sprays of leaves – abandoned and trampled – were scattered in their thousands along the footpaths and byways leading back to the station and other points of departure.

If the local population objected to this wholesale pruning of the countryside, they did not show it. Should visitors wish to pick flowers, so be it, they would soon grow again. Holidaymakers represented an important source of revenue, they were to be welcomed, not warned off. As for the practical measures taken to ensure a smooth reception, these were described by an elderly lady when recalling her childhood before the First World War:

> "I was once told," she informed us, "the reason why the platform at Hassocks is so long (which indeed it is) was because of the length of the trains bringing visitors."

Tens of thousands of people, according to this same lady, descended on the district during the season. And if that was the case, it was surely the sight of so many potential customers milling about with their arms full of bluebells and their pockets full of money, that persuaded Mr Frederick John Wellman, a Brighton restaurant keeper, with premises in Prince Albert Street, that good investment opportunities could still be found in the Pleasure Gardens business. He was absolutely right, it was the golden age of pleasure! The high summer of the Edwardian era! The famous Victoria Gardens were going great guns at Burgess Hill. The Chinese Gardens were riding the crest of the wave at Hurstpierpoint, and a host of smaller establishments including Webbs Park, The Friars Oak, and the Hassocks Hotel were all drawing large and regular crowds. Yet despite the glut of

Frederick John Wellman

Florence Lucy Wellman, née Waldegrave

attractions, there was plenty of room for more and Hassocks, with its all important railway station, was the ideal spot, if a suitable location could be found.

Frederick Wellman was born in 1875 at Goldstone Mews, Shirley Street, Hove, and educated at the local church school in George Street. On completing his studies, he joined the Merchant Navy, and then later, the P & O Line, during which time he travelled the world. On leaving the service, he married Florence Lucy Waldegrave, the wedding taking place in 1899, after which the young couple commenced married life running the restaurant referred to earlier.

Although not a native of the area, Wellman was no stranger to Hassocks and visited the district frequently in order to see his parents who lived at 34

Keymer Road, Hassocks – The two white topped gateposts that can just be seen behind the cyclist's head, denote the entrance to Balchin's Nursery (now Grand Avenue) although interestingly there appears to be no dip in the kerbstones at that point. This could possibly mean that the approach was purely pedestrian and that in those days, heavy vehicles were required to use Orchard Lane in order to reach the premises?

73

The entrance to the Orchard Tea Gardens.

The driveway (now Grand Avenue) looking north

Parklands Road. His father, also named Frederick Wellman, was a Dorset man, and deserves more than the brief mention we are able to provide, for he was a much decorated soldier, a Crimean veteran who saw action at the siege of Sebastopol, and later fought in the Indian Mutiny. How long he and his wife, Mary, lived in Mid Sussex, we do not know, but it was probably for most of his retirement, and as we have said, young Frederick visited them regularly.

At the time in question (the opening years of the 20th century) a long established firm in the vicinity was a company called W. Balchin & Sons. They were florists and seedsmen, who in addition to having similar businesses in Brighton and Hove, also owned a nursery where Grand Avenue now stands. Many of their local staff were housed in Parklands Road, which possibly suggests that Mr Wellman senior might have worked there too? If that was the case, he and his fellow employees were in a for rude shock! For in 1906, or thereabouts, the Directors – for reasons best known to themselves – decided to trim their assets, and as a result closed down the Hassocks branch, and placed it on the market.

Whether anticipated or not, this was the opportunity Mr Wellman had been waiting for. We know from a first hand source[1] that he had spent a considerable time studying the way in which the Victoria Gardens operated, and in consequence was longing to put his own ideas into practice. So without a moment's hesitation, he acquired the freehold of the nursery, took up the occupancy of Scotland House (the residence thereon) and began the job of converting the grounds into a holiday resort.

Putting commercial pressure to one side, it must have been a pleasant task, for the area was exceedingly lovely. The tastefully grouped trees and shrubs and the immaculate lawns on either side of the driveway heading from Keymer Road to the Gardens, was a superb feature in itself. In early spring, the banks were massed with drifts of sweet smelling violets and shiny yellow celandines, followed later by primroses, anemones, ladysmock and bluebells, while on a more formal note, dazzling displays of cultivated flowers, such as tulips and polyanthus, geraniums and lilies were planted out in beds artistically arranged to catch the visitors' eye.

There was only one practical drawback to the site, a lack of boating facilities, but this was easily overcome, for the western boundary of the property was formed by the Herring Stream, the well-known Hassocks water way that flows beneath Spitalford Bridge. So acting on the advice of his friendly rival, Edwin Street, Mr Wellman provided a month or so's work for the unemployed, and they excavated a shallow hole, about one and a half acres in extent, flooded it from the brook and thereby created a splendid lake.

While the digging was in progress, the attractions one would expect to find in a successful pleasure gardens were swiftly being installed. There were rows of swingboats, ordinary plank-swings, see-saws and slides, roundabouts and giant strides. Donkeys were stabled at the premises, so that those who fancied their chances would be able to make a tour of the grounds, while the less adventurous could follow in goat carts. Tennis courts were constructed. A huge playing field was laid out for cricket, football, and other outdoor games.

[1] Ivy Dudeney (née Street)

The boating lake, prior to the First World War

Archery was available for aspiring bowmen, and most importantly, in the event of inclement weather, a vast covered area was provided for visitors to pursue a variety of indoor amusements.

A commodious dining hall, gas lit and capable of seating four hundred guests was constructed, and this building also doubled as a ballroom and was used for a various entertainments.

The Helter-Skelter

However, the outstanding feature was undoubtedly the helter-skelter, this was a massive edifice and quite literally towered over everything else in the neighbourhood. There was hardly a bedroom in the village that was safe from the enquiring eyes of those prepared to make the climb, and after satisfying their curiosity, these Edwardian voyeurs enthroned upon little cushions, slid swiftly back to the ground where they sought other diversions. One life-long Hassocks resident told us:

> You could hire a telescope, it added to the cost but was worth every penny, because from the top there was a breathtaking view of the South Downs stretching all the way from Wolstonbury to Blackcap. Oldlands Mill seemed so close you really felt that you could reach out and touch it! and they said that the people at the Burgess Hill Hydro (Franklands) used to keep their curtains drawn at the weekends. I knew a girl who was in service there, and she told me that sometimes you could see lights flashing from the top of the Helter-Skelter. Like army heliographs, she said.

Mr Wellman's venture, which was named the Orchard Tea Gardens, opened to the public in 1908. It was a latecomer to the trade, but nevertheless got off to a roaring start. Like the Victoria Gardens, it was a teetotal establishment, and as such, appealed strongly to the various Sunday schools and church social organisations that were predominant at the time. Despite the considerable business they brought, these groups had been strangely neglected by the holiday resorts. Edwin Street had spotted the potential back in 1897, and as a result enjoyed eleven years of unparalleled prosperity. His was an example that the Hassocks proprietor was pleased to follow, and it proved to be a wise decision.

In a historical compilation called *Backyard Brighton*, which was published by QueenSpark Books, an unnamed author recalled a childhood outing to the Gardens in their early days.

> Our treat was the Sunday School Treat. For weeks before we used to try and save up a few pence and each Grandmother would give us a penny. We had to take our own dinner which was usually corn beef or jam sandwiches, a bottle of drink which was usually a halfpenny worth of lemonade powder put in a bottle of water. We also had to take an enamel mug with our name tape sewn round the handle.

> We would meet at St Peter's Church and march up Trafalgar Street to the station where we would get a train to Hassocks Tea Gardens. The swings were free, but the other rides were a halfpenny or a penny. At four o'clock a whistle would blow when we would all rush to the trestle tables and forms that had been put up at one end of the Gardens. That is when we used our mugs, they would come round with big pots of tea with the milk and sugar already in it, just too bad if you didn't take sugar. Then they would come round with the sandwiches which were always strawberry jam. You could have four of those, then they would come round with the cakes which were a halfpenny currant bun and a penny iced cake each. After tea, you could go and play, and there was always a rush for the free swings as everybody had spent their money by then. Parents were allowed to come, but had to pay for themselves on the train etc. At six o' clock another whistle would blow and the children would know it was time to go home. We would line up to be counted to make sure nobody was missing, then we would be marched to Hassocks station to catch the train home. The older children were allowed to go home from the station, but the younger ones would be marched back to St Peter's Church, where their parents were waiting to collect them. I suppose we must have had some wet days on our treat, but I can only remember one, and that happened on the way home.

With a young family to raise and a thriving enterprise to run, the early secure years at Hassocks must have flashed by for the Wellman's. They, in common with so many others, could hardly have anticipated the forthcoming carnage and chaos that was destined to change the world for ever. When, in 1914, the dreadful moment came, and war was declared against Germany, Mr Wellman was not found wanting. Although aged 39, and therefore too old to be considered for the fighting forces, he immediately enlisted into the Ambulance Brigade, and in that unit, served throughout the conflict in the battle zones of Italy and France. Recognition of his outstanding service was contained in a document described as an 'Illuminated Address of Thanks' which was officially presented to him by a grateful French Government.

Birds Eye View Orchard G...

Looking west over the grounds towards the railway embankment at the foot of Woodsland Road

A Sunday afternoon at Hassocks

In the meantime, his wife continued to run the Tea Gardens as well as bringing up their three children, and although she received assistance from her husband's elderly parents, it could have been no easy job, for despite the harsh times, business continued to flourish and demanded her every attention.

It was hardly the business she originally envisaged. Sunday School parties and similar organisations still came of course, but as well as these, large groups of wounded war veterans travelled up from the Brighton hospitals. They were surely bitter-sweet occasions? Charabancs full of service men, some terribly injured, arrived at the Gardens where they received a hero's welcome and the freedom of the grounds, the day invariably ending with a concert or a sing-song. These musical entertainments were hugely popular, especially during the long summer evenings, when the soldiers dressed in hospital 'blues' gathered round a piano on the lawn and sang popular ballads of the time. They sang with great gusto, and after concluding with the National Anthem, accorded Mrs Wellman, her staff and helpers, three hearty cheers. Then amidst much laughter and banter, the men, pockets bulging with sweets and cigarettes (gifts from the villagers) boarded the waiting transport and were driven off.

"We were all very quiet after they had gone," one lady recalled. "More than anything else, the sight of those poor wretches, covered in bandages and limping along on crutches, made you realise the futility and horror of war. Yet they never complained. They thought they were lucky to be alive. It made me want to cry!"

Wounded soldiers from a Brighton hospital visiting the Gardens in 1916

The Evening Concert

After peace was declared and the men came home, Mr Wellman, for reasons we have been unable to establish, sold the Gardens and returned to the coast, and in so doing, severed his connection with the business of pleasure. Before we too move on, a brief look at his later achievements will give some measure of the sheer vitality of the man.

Apparently at an earlier stage of his career – we know not when – he formed what was to become a lifelong friendship with the great Brighton philanthropist, Lewis C. Cohen, an influential figure, who happened to be a member of the board of the Brighton and Sussex Building Society, and when that society was reorganised in 1929, Mr Wellman became vice-chairman. Being a great advocate of amalgamation, he strongly supported the merger, which in due course saw a number of societies unite under the collective heading of the 'Alliance' and in 1952, he was elected chairman. He also found time to serve as chairman of the Brighton Board of Guardians as well as the General Purposes Committee, the Finance Committee, and the Haywards Heath Mental Hospital Visitors Committee. In addition, he was the vice-chairman of the Warren Farm School, and as a by-the-by sat as a magistrate in Brighton for well nigh twenty years.

An important, yet strangely neglected figure as far as the history of Hassocks is concerned, Mr Wellman died in 1959 in his eighty-third year, not from sheer exhaustion as one might have supposed, but as a result of an infection he contracted whilst undergoing medical treatment for an abscess in the shoulder.

The new owner of the Orchard Tea Gardens was a retired accountant and inventor from Mortlake, Villeroy Corney Doubleday. His family had local connections insofar that his father had once resided at a rather handsome premises called Tower House, which prior to demolition, stood at the corner of Silverdale Road, Burgess Hill – opposite to Hoadley's departmental store.

Although elderly, Mr Doubleday was an extremely energetic man, he was also wealthy and utterly determined to transform the venue into the most attractive and up-to-date resort in Sussex. The project became his primary interest, and he delighted to lavish on it all the considerable resources at his command. He spent, for instance, over £3,000 (a vast amount in those days) on concrete alone. This included a new base for the lake – which readers may recall was nearly two acres in extent – and a cemented cycle track. The existing buildings were upgraded, and an extra tea room, with a marvellous verandah overlooking the lake was constructed for the use of adults only. In addition, he built what was described as an elevated "rest" and observation room which commanded a superb view over the whole of the grounds, while a further 5,000 square feet containing swings etc was roofed over to serve as a dry play area in case of rain. There was a shop stocked with a good variety of toys, as well as souvenirs and confectionery. This fronted onto a large workshed, the interior of which, pervaded by the aroma of linseed oil, was the domain of Mr J. Morris, a carpenter from Parklands Road. During the winter months, the boats were brought up from the lake and stored in this shed, where Mr Morris caulked the seams, preserved the timbers, and forgive the pun – kept them shipshape!

Villeroy Corney Doubleday

The Lake, during Mr Doubleday's term as proprietor

The outside dining area

Mr Doubleday made a slight alteration to the name of the venue, changing it from the Orchard Tea Gardens to the Orchard Pleasure Gardens. Then, despite some initial trouble from Brighton roughs, which was swiftly contained by the police, business boomed, and during the post war years, crowds continued to descend on Hassocks in numbers as large as ever. The individual entrance fee was raised to threepence (just over 1p) but in the case of large groups, it remained at the rate of five shillings (25p) per 100 persons. Everyone prospered, with the possible exception of local flower sellers, whose business was largely usurped by a gentleman from Albourne (Mr Starley) who sold sweet peas from a motor cycle and sidecar.

The range of amusements was increased. Visitors discovered that a Chairoplane Roundabout, as well as eight rows of Toboggan Slides with rails and trolleys had been added to the existing attractions. On top of which was the Bicycle Roundabout, Hoop-la stall, and various side-shows that had been introduced by the Shippobottam's, while down on the lake, a brand new motor boat provided trips for those who were disinclined to row.

Mr Doubleday's wife, Rhoda, took on the job of catering, and although hot meals were not on the menu, cold luncheons were available at one shilling

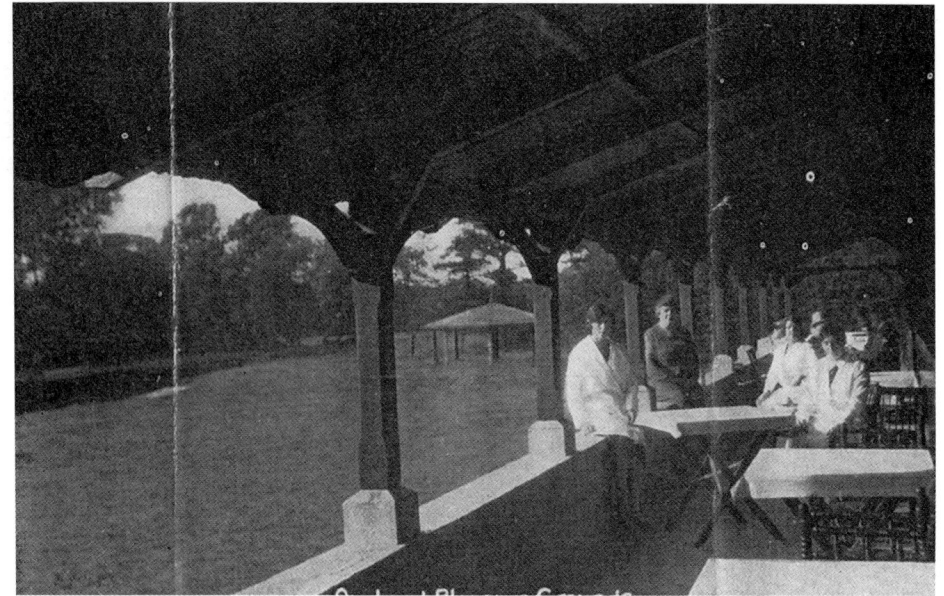

The Verandah (overlooking the Lake)

The toboggan slides

and sixpence (7.5p) and two shillings (10p) Adult teas, which consisted of white and brown bread and butter, jam, lettuce and fancy cakes, cost one shilling and one penny (just over 5p). Children's teas, which were smaller portions without the lettuce, cost eightpence (approx 3.5p). The bread and cakes were supplied by Holloways Bakery from Burgess Hill.

In a letter to the *Mid Sussex Times*, which referred to the days when, as a young woman, she had been employed at the Orchard Pleasure Gardens, a Mrs J. Sunderland recalled:

> I worked, with others, in the kitchens, where we catered for the large parties of schoolchildren who came on outings from London. Towards the end of the day, they all trooped into the huge tea room, where the long trestle tables spread with white cloths, had been laid with plates of sliced bread and cakes, dishes of jam, big brown tea pots and hundreds of cups and saucers and plates.

> We were kept on the run, replenishing the rapidly vanishing food. The country air certainly sharpened their appetite! The chatter was deafening. When everyone had eaten their fill, the teacher in charge made a little speech of thanks for all of our hard work, and we were given an enormous cheer.

The main approach to the grounds was substantially altered. Gone were the famous white posts with the pergola-shaped tops, gone too was the arched sign and trim hedgerow. In their place a pair of beautifully crafted oak gates, a matching wicket gate and a smart wooden fence, set in semi-circular fashion, combined to make a most attractive entrance. The little kiosk in which Mr Wellman senior used to greet the customers was still retained but in a slightly different position. However, all of this faded into insignificance, for what really caught the eye was the spectacle of two field guns, positioned either side of the driveway with their barrels pointing towards the upper storeys of Parkmore Terrace! Such was their effect that a stranger to the district could have been excused for thinking he was passing an army barracks instead of a holiday resort.

Mid Sussex would seem to have been a veritable mecca for inventors. In our books, *From Pyecombe to Cuckfield* and *Albourne to Ditchling*, we have referred to such well-known names as Magnus Volk, John Saxby, Sidney Hole and James Starley, a worthy company indeed and Villeroy Doubleday certainly warrants inclusion in their ranks. He was an experienced engineer and had acquired respect at the highest level for the

Although of poor quality, this photograph clearly shows the alterations made to the entrance of the Orchard Gardens in Mr Doubleday's time. The field guns can be seen behind the fence on either side of the main gates.

shrewd and imaginative way in which he dealt with apparently insoluble problems. One of his inventions, a field gun fired by compressed air, was accepted by the War Office, and it is likely, though not certain, that the guns at Hassocks may have been prototypes of this.

A further example of his genius was reported in the *Mid Sussex Times* in 1927, when under the heading, 'Remarkable Invention at Hassocks', it stated:

> A wonderful invention which promises to have a world wide effect on the musical arrangements at cinemas, dance halls and even theatres and churches, has just been patented by a Brighton man and demonstrated for the first time at Hassocks.

> The story behind the invention is briefly as follows:

> For over three years, Mr V. C. Doubleday of the Orchard Pleasure Gardens, Hassocks, had been trying to get electrical experts to

The Bicycle Roundabout, which was one of the amusements run by the Shippobottam family. Mrs Shippobottam is thought to be the lady in the foreground and Scotland House can just be seen on the extreme right.

take up his idea that gramophones could be vastly amplified by electricity. He was turned down by practically every firm he approached, being told that even if such a thing was possible, the results would be most unsatisfactory.

Having met with nothing but discouragement in London and several other big cities he visited, Mr Doubleday eventually got in touch with Mr B. Elkin, a young wireless engineer of 2, Cumberland Road, Brighton, who had been working on the very same thing for some two years. The two decided to cooperate and after many experiments, Mr Elkin succeeded beyond the most sanguine hopes of either himself or his friend. People at Hassocks, some of them living a quarter of a mile from the Orchard Pleasure Gardens, were mystified by hearing strains of music by brass bands, orchestras and church organs at most unexpected hours, and it was not until Mr Doubleday invited a few friends to hear 'The Elkestra', as the invention had been named, that the mystery was solved.

The visitors were shown into the spacious tea room and the building was suddenly flooded with music. To the amazement of those who were not in the know, it was pointed out that the huge volume of sound proceeded from an adjacent building. The perfection of the notes, especially the bass ones which wireless does not transmit, were remarkable and there was a complete absence of atmospherics and of scratching sounds usually associated with a gramophone. The inventor told the *Mid Sussex Times* representative that the machine was capable of amplifying up to 35,000 times, and that the power of the transmission is about 20 watts. Any distortion due to excessive loudness is indicated on a dial and can be remedied immediately by turning a knob. it costs about £100 including a gramophone.

The apparatus is exceedingly simple to work and is completely foolproof, and among other advantages, it has a fading out arrangement whereby it can be switched from one gramophone to another in a fraction of a second. Vocal and instrumental music comes through with equal facility and the invention so delighted the few cinema proprietors who have so far been privileged to hear it, that they gave orders for one on the spot.

All in all it must be said that the Doubledays led a full life and contributed much to the benefit of those about them, yet they had known tragedy. In 1918, their son, a lad of thirteen, died whilst in a diabetic coma. Their grief was partly eased by the birth of another boy the following year who was christened Robin.

Mrs Rhoda Doubleday and Robin Doubleday

Villeroy Doubleday died in 1932. He was in his 76th year, and with his death, Mid Sussex lost a popular and famous resident. His widow continued to run the Gardens for a while, but with Robin showing little interest in the business, her own committment waned, and it came as no surprise when in 1935, she sold the land for development, and moved away. It appeared however, that her fondness for the area was greater than she realised, for a few years later, she returned to the village and took up residence in a property at The Close, near to her old home. What happiness she experienced in coming back was sadly short lived, for tragedy struck again, this time in 1944, when Robin Doubleday, now a young man of twenty-five, perished at Arnhem. His mother never recovered from the shock, and shortly after, she too had gone.

Time marches on, as they say, and those who can recall the days when Hassocks was a popular holiday resort are now few in number. Scotland House and Orchard Lane still bear mute witness to a past age, but otherwise nothing is left to show that the Gardens ever existed. All has been buried beneath bricks and mortar, which brings us to the end of the story – save for one closing reflection:

In this modern age, visits to exotic locations are commonplace for a sophisticated public with money to spend, time to spare, and a tourism industry to support. Yet, as we have learned, not long ago, a trip to the countryside with perhaps a boating pool, some swings and roundabouts, and the prospects of strawberry jam for tea, was all that most people could aspire to in the way of a summer vacation.

The proprietors referred to in this book provided such attractions in abundance, they were pioneers and in the nicest way proved that business and pleasure really could be mixed. For this reason alone, we hope that they will not be entirely forgotten.

The end of the day

Sources

A Rail Road Trip to Shoreham and a Visit to the Swiss Gardens – R. Sickelmore

Backyard Brighton, published by QueenSpark Books

Birds of Sussex – William Borrer

Brighton – Osbert Sitwell and Margaret Barton

Brighton in the Olden Time – John George Bishop

Devil's Dyke in Old Picture Postcards – Ernest Ryman

Downland Pathways – A. Hadrian Allcroft

Edwin Street and the Victoria Pleasure Gardens – Mark Dudeney and Eileen Hallett

Esther Waters – George Moore

Guide to Brighton and the Devil's Dyke – D. B. Friend

Hassocks and Keymer Talkabout

Highways and Byways in Sussex – E.V. Lucas

Life in Brighton – Clifford Musgrave

New Brighton Guide

Sickelmore's Select Views of Brighton

Shoreham Glories (In Scraps and Stories) – "William"

Sussex – Wilfrid Ball

Sussex County Magazine

Sussex Industrial History

Sussex Rendevous – R. Thurston Hopkins

The Book of Brighton, As It Was and As It Is. And Talkee-Talkee

The Brighton Gazette

The Locomotive

The Mid Sussex Times

The Old Century – Mark Dudeney (unpublished)

The Story of Shoreham – Henry Cheal

The Sussex Agricultural Express

Also Published by Mid-Sussex Books

Edwin Street and the Victoria Pleasure Gardens
Mark Dudeney and Eileen Hallett

"A fascinating peep into the turn of the century fun park"
– Brighton and Hove Leader

"The book's a winner"
– Mid Sussex Times

"The definitive book on the subject"
– West Sussex Gazette

"A thoroughly good read and highly recommended"
– Antique Amusements Magazine

From Pyecombe to Cuckfield: With Stops Along the Way
Mark Dudeney and Eileen Hallett

"This delightful book"
– Mid Sussex Leader

"Fascinating tales and anecdotes which bring the period to life"
– Mid Sussex Times

Albourne to Ditchling: Along the Greensand Ridge
Mark Dudeney and Eileen Hallett

"Packed with good tales, is attractively illustrated, and has stunning and historic photographs
– Mid Sussex Times

"Highly entertaining"
– Sussex Express

"This is a book to enjoy or maybe give as a present – if you can part with it
– Hassocks and Keymer Talkabout

"A celebration of the rural district Mid Sussex used to be"
– West Sussex gazette

"An excellent journey through time"
– Evening Argus

In Preparation

The Old Century
Mark Dudeney